ISIS: THE HEART OF TERROR

EUGENE BACH

Unless otherwise indicated, Scripture quotations are taken from *The Holy Bible, English Standard Version,* © 2000, 2001, 1995 by Crossway Bibles, a division of Good News Publishers. Used by permission. All rights reserved. Scripture quotations marked (ASV) are taken from the American Standard Edition of the Revised Version of the Holy Bible. Scripture quotations marked (KJV) are taken from the King James Version of the Holy Bible. Scripture quotations marked (NIV) are taken from the *Holy Bible, New International Version*®, NIV®, © 1973, 1978, 1984 by the International Bible Society. Used by permission of Zondervan. All rights reserved.

Note: Boldface type in Scripture quotations indicates the author's emphasis.

Unless otherwise indicated, Koranic quotations are taken from http://www.quran.com.

ISIS, THE HEART OF TERROR:
The Unexpected Response Bringing Hope for Peace

ISBN: 978-1-62911-386-9
eBook ISBN: 978-1-62911-387-6
Printed in the United States of America

Whitaker House
1030 Hunt Valley Circle
New Kensington, PA 15068
www.whitakerhouse.com

Library of Congress Cataloging-in-Publication Data (Pending)

1 2 3 4 5 6 7 8 9 10 W 21 20 19 18 17 16 15

Contents

Preface

Unlike other books about ISIS (the Islamic State of Iraq and Syria), this work is written from the viewpoint of the Chinese missionary movement known as "Back to Jerusalem." The Chinese underground church has a vision to take the gospel message to Iraq and Syria, and it is crossing paths with ISIS.[1] I am not an expert on ISIS; neither am I an expert on the situation in the Middle East. But I have worked with the underground church in China for more than fifteen years.

I also spend a lot of my time working in moderate Muslim countries like Turkey, Malaysia, and Indonesia. I often find myself in the United Arab Emirates (UAE) and Pakistan. I have spent time on the ground in Iraq and Syria. I have even taken some time to go skiing with Muslim friends in the mountains of Iran. Unlike most foreigners traveling in those countries, I am not insulated from the local population by Western hotel accommodations and hot spots that act as tourist bubbles, allowing one to observe the locals merely from a distance. Being involved with grassroots missions has thrown me into the fires of cultural immersion of every country where we work.

Therefore, more than just evaluating and describing the leadership and tactics of the infamous terror group known as ISIS, this book will examine the dark heart of Islamic jihadists and what Christians can do in response to their war. It will show how you can help to alleviate one of the largest man-made humanitarian disasters in the world today.

In *ISIS, The Heart of Terror,* you will learn what ISIS is, how it came into being, and what its vision for the future includes. You will read horror stories about ISIS and its goal of establishing an Islamic state through jihad. You will read testimonies from persecuted Christians who have fled their homes, lost their family members, and are now on the run from ISIS. You will also hear from the family of a pastor who, at the time of this writing, is imprisoned in Iran, and whom ISIS has issued an order to kill.

In these pages, you will learn about the unique way God is moving among Chinese missionaries to provide Christian materials in Iraq and Syria, and, for the first time, to share the gospel with displaced minorities who previously had been largely unreachable. These exclusive chapters will take you undercover to see how Chinese missionaries, rather than living in fear of ISIS, plan to use cutting-edge technology to "target" ISIS members with the gospel of Jesus Christ! "Are the members of ISIS any different from the apostle Paul?" asked one Chinese pastor who is involved in the outreach operation. "Didn't Jesus die for them, as well?"

Can the terror tactics of ISIS be stopped? Can missionaries help communities that have been displaced by ISIS, and share the gospel message with unreached people groups that have never before been accessible? Can underground Chinese missionaries really change the hearts of ISIS members with the good news of Jesus Christ?

The future peace and stability of Israel, the presence of Christianity in the Middle East, and the current way of life for people living in the Western world may well rest on how we respond to the present crisis created by ISIS.

ONE

The Western World Meets ISIS

The startling video that was shown first on YouTube and then quickly spread to other Internet sites in August 2014 reminded many people of that dreadful day, September 11, 2001.

It was the video that few really wanted to see or to believe. American journalist James Foley was on his knees in the desert sand wearing an orange jumpsuit and facing a camera. A masked, black-clad Muslim jihadist stood behind him. "I call on my friends, family, and loved ones to rise up against my real killers, the U.S. government," Foley said in a scripted voice as he looked into the camera.

James Foley was gaunt and bald, his head shaven. His orange jumpsuit was a replica of those worn by prisoners in Guantánamo Bay, Cuba. Sweat glistened on his forehead as he continued speaking, pausing between phrases and sentences. "I wish I had more time. I wish I could have had the hope of…seeing my family once again. I guess, all in all, I wish I wasn't American."[2] Those were his last known words.

Many people watched the video in shock. They all knew what was coming, but few expected it to actually happen. The black-clad

Muslim jihadist who stood behind Foley, holding on to his orange shirt, became commonly known as "Jihadi John."

Unfortunately, Foley was not being videotaped for the purpose of extracting a ransom from his family or his government. The Muslim jihadists were not demanding money. Foley was being used solely as a prop to get the world's attention and to help deliver a message of doom.

Jihadi John was dressed in a robe and a mask (reminiscent of a sloppy Japanese ninja), an outfit that is now synonymous with terrorist fighters. He stood in front of the camera with his feet shoulder-width apart, wearing tan, military-issued desert boots and a brown leather shoulder holster. He spoke calmly in an accent that one might hear in any Middle Eastern community in London today—not exactly British, not exactly Middle Eastern.

Jihadi John pointed his knife squarely at the camera and said,

> ...any aggression toward the Islamic State is an aggression towards Muslims from all walks of life who have accepted the Islamic caliphate as their leadership. So any attempt by you, Obama, to deny the Muslims their rights of living in safety under the Islamic caliphate will result in the bloodshed of your people.[3]

Then he walked behind Foley, whose face was as tense as steel.

The captive tightly shut his eyes, as if to mentally brace himself for what was about to happen. Who knows how many times he had gone through mock killings before this day? (Like James Foley, Amanda Lindhout was a journalist who was kidnapped by Islamic jihadists. She was held captive for fifteen months. In her autobiography, *A House in the Sky: A Memoir,* she describes the mock executions she was subjected to on a regular basis. They were demoralizing and took away any sense of security.)

Foley's body was erect and stiff. Jihadi John calmly reached around Foley's head and put his right hand over his mouth. The jihadist clinched his fingers under James's chin, gripped his nose area with his thumb, and held his palm over his mouth to muffle any screams. With his left hand, Jihadi John retrieved his knife and held it firmly to Foley's throat; then he began to crudely saw back and forth into the jugular. James's lips formed an *o* as he took one last breath.

Seconds later, Foley's body was shown lying on the desert sand, head detached and resting on the small of his back. A successful young American journalist who, only recently, had been full of life was now lifeless and covered in blood.

YouTube was slow to remove the gruesome video. Many people, myself included, had already seen the video before it was taken down. The problem was that the video could not be unseen. The gruesome images could not be erased from people's minds. And—even worse—the killing of James Foley could never be undone.

The horrifying act that many people had a hard time processing was shared on social media. Suddenly, instead of the regular postings of recipes and family vacation photos, Facebook was full of people's reactions to the beheading of James Foley.

The Middle Eastern quandary of radical Islam and violence was once again confronting the Western world—and it was at the gates of the Western church. The feelings of intimidation that arose in many Americans after watching the beheading of a fellow countryman hit closer to home than most wanted to acknowledge.

What Is ISIS?

To many people, Jihadi John represents a new threat from a relatively unknown group called ISIS. The graphic video prompted many to ask, for the first time, "What is ISIS?" "Where did it come from?" and "What does it want?"

If I were to ask a Christian in Iraq who had fled from his home for fear of his life what ISIS is, his answer would be much different from that of a tourist in Paris. If I were to ask someone on a subway in downtown Manhattan what ISIS is, the passenger would answer much differently than would a typical passenger riding the Cross-Harbour ferry in Hong Kong.

"Who is ISIS?" asked a friendly lady sitting beside me on a flight from Baton Rouge to Dallas in September 2014. She had been peeking over my shoulder as I wrote notes for this book. She worked for the Federal Emergency Management Agency (FEMA) in the United States, and she had just come from a FEMA seminar called "Preparing Before Disaster."

"I have heard of ISIS on the news, and now everyone is talking about them, but I really don't understand who they are," she said as she pointed to the screen on my computer. "They scare me, which is silly, because I don't even know who they are."

Similar words are echoed in many homes throughout the Western world today, indicating ISIS's successful propaganda campaign.

It seems as if the ISIS threat should be worlds away, in places that are never mentioned on the news. But the terror organization is now a common concern for everyone. The world is not ready for the ISIS threat—but it has arrived. Cities like Mosul in Iraq and Abu Kamal in Syria may not be places many tourists visit or would ever care to visit, but cities like London, Paris, New York, and Sydney are, and they are now on the ISIS list of targets.

Some of the information presented in this book might initially come across as sensationalistic or even as fearmongering;

but, before you jump to either of those conclusions, consider the following points, which we will discuss in more detail later:

- ISIS is more extreme and brutal than al-Qaeda, as hard as that might be to believe. In fact, ISIS is so brutal that al-Qaeda has tried to distance itself from it. Imagine that for a moment. Osama bin Laden actually felt that the tactics ISIS used were too extreme.
- ISIS is the wealthiest terrorist group in the history of the world. Never before has a terrorist organization had access to so many resources. ISIS controls many large oil and gas fields, and it has the expertise and security needed to transport and sell both the oil and the gas.
- ISIS controls a vast military that has both training and experience. It has been able to obtain much of its firepower and equipment from conquered military units in both Syria and Iraq. Much of the equipment it has acquired is from the U.S. military.
- ISIS is one of the fiercest enemies the world has ever faced. Members of ISIS have been hardened over the years and have acquired much experience in previous battles against the United States, Syria, and Iraq. Most terrorist groups attack only soft targets, such as unarmed communities, children, schools, bus stops, and so forth; but ISIS attacks both soft and hard targets, such as militaries.
- ISIS is seeking to obtain nuclear material that can be weaponized. If successful, it will be the first terrorist group to obtain nuclear capabilities while having a budget large enough to employ it.
- ISIS has recruited many foreign fighters from Canada, the US, Australia, New Zealand, and Europe. ISIS fighters are able to take the battle from the fields of Syria and Iraq to

Western soil. Al-Qaeda members, who are forced to obtain visas and are often from countries that are already on watch lists, do not have this ability.

As of the writing of this book, according to the *Wall Street Journal,* ISIS controls territory in both northern and eastern Syria and western Iraq that amounts to 12,000 square miles of contiguous area, roughly the size of Belgium.[4]

Unlike al-Qaeda, which does not have a capital city, a headquarters, or an official governing structure for overseeing communities, ISIS has a capital with buildings and is able to provide public services. Many of the buildings that ISIS uses as governing posts are those of former churches that they have taken over and painted black. In many ways, ISIS has indeed become an Islamic state. It has been able to carve out a small piece of land that it runs as an independent region.

This terrorist organization already enforces dress codes for women, holds court trials for criminals, and sets rules for schools. Enforcement officers patrol the streets and ensure Islamic order. In fact, in many of the schools, ISIS has even set up the curriculum for the students. "The Islamic State's Caliphate has now established a single economic system and currency for all territories under its control."[5] Its army has taken over Mosul, one of Iraq's largest cities, and it is also on the border of Baghdad.

Those who are part of ISIS are asking the world to give them "freedom," or, essentially, to leave them alone so that they can take over both Syria and Iraq and establish a society under the Islamic caliphate.[6] Eventually, after conquering the Middle East, ISIS will consolidate its strength and immediately turn its focus on other countries, including those in the West.

ISIS is not an organization of competing ideas. It is made up of single-minded radicals who insist that they are right, and who will use death to silence anyone who disagrees. Again, ISIS is possibly the most brutal terrorist organization the world has ever seen. Its growth is alarming, and the magnitude and breadth of its success have caught many world leaders by surprise, including President Barack Obama.

The U.S. president grossly underestimated the jihadist group. For example, speaking of ISIS in January 2014 during an interview with the *New Yorker,* Obama said, "The analogy we use around here sometimes, and I think is accurate, is if a jayvee team puts on Lakers uniforms that doesn't make them Kobe Bryant."[7] Later that year, he seemed to better understand the threat, but addressing it was another matter. In a speech about ISIS that he delivered on September 4, 2014, he said, "We do not have a strategy yet."[8]

He was not the only person to be caught by surprise. Because of the rapid growth of ISIS and most people's lack of knowledge regarding the organization, many people find themselves scrambling for information about a terror group that is now threatening their lives.

To get an idea of the group's swift growth, consider the following: In the early months of 2014, more British citizens joined the ranks of ISIS than joined the British Army.[9]

The brutality of ISIS is beyond anything that most people can imagine, and its members wield that violence against Christians, Jews, Kurds, Yazidis, and even fellow Muslims, such as the Shiites, who do not agree with fundamentalist Sunni Islam.

In both Syria and Iraq, ISIS has attacked tens of thousands of Christians and executed their leaders. Many of these leaders were marched out to dig the very trenches they were later buried in. Some leaders were even crucified on crosses. Not even children are immune to these attacks. Some of them have been beheaded; others have been sold as slaves.

The Christians whom ISIS does not immediately kill are given the choice of one of three chilling ultimatums: convert to Islam, pay *jizya*—an Islamic tax imposed on non-Muslims—or die. To ensure efficiency, ISIS members walk through towns and mark Christian homes with the Arabic letter *n*, ن, signifying "Nazarene," which they consider a pejorative term for Christians.

Moreover, while terrorist organizations like Hamas and al-Qaeda may not be working directly with ISIS, they still target Israel and the Western Christian world. Even though these three organizations are separate, it would be a mistake to think of their efforts and vision as different from one another. They are unified in their faith, their hatred, and their terror tactics.

ISIS, along with Hamas and al-Qaeda, desires to wage jihad until Israel is destroyed and a caliphate is established. From the perspective of ISIS, these goals are nonnegotiable; a peaceful compromise does not exist, and peaceful coexistence with Israel is not an option.

ISIS now attempts to annihilate huge populations of people groups, and the momentum is in their favor.

After the Holocaust, the world vowed that it would never again fail to take action to prevent genocide. Recently, I walked through the killing fields of Cambodia with my youngest son. As we gazed upon the "killing tree"—where hundreds, if not thousands, of babies were killed—and walked through the mass grave site of so many Cambodian Christians, whose bone fragments are still scattered all around, I could not help but think that, in every generation, some person and/or organization arises that becomes a killing force in the world. To counter this threat, every generation must have a group of Christian believers who will not accept this situation and will arise and put a stop to it.

ISIS must be stopped, and, God willing, it will be stopped; but the question my generation will have to answer to my young son's generation is, "Who stopped ISIS?"

The Radicalization of ISIS Leader Al-Baghdadi

The photograph of a black-hooded man standing on a brown cardboard box that was flashed across news sites around the world became an international symbol of torture. It was a shocking image that then president George W. Bush could not ignore.

The photo was among those that CNN released on May 1, 2004, of the American-run Abu Ghraib prison in Iraq. In addition to the picture of the man in the hooded mask standing on a box, his outstretched arms attached to electrical wires, was another photograph of a woman holding a leash wrapped around an Iraqi prisoner's neck as he lay on the ground. Another was of a group of nearly naked prisoners who were stacked in the form of a pyramid on the ground. These images were burned into the minds of many people who viewed them.

Because of the outrage that followed the release of the photos, the United States began to transfer prisoners from Abu Ghraib to Camp Bucca, another American-run prison in Umm Qasr, Iraq.

The new arrivals from Abu Ghraib did not know it then, but they were sharing a prison with someone who would one day be the most wanted man in the world, the self-appointed caliphate and leader of ISIS, which, as we have noted, is the wealthiest and arguably the most powerful terrorist organization in history.

The name Abu Bakr al-Baghdadi does not roll off the tongue as easily as does the name Osama bin Laden; consequently, his name is not yet as synonymous with evil. However, he is just as dangerous, if not more dangerous, than Osama bin Laden ever was. And, to fully understand the history and characteristics of ISIS, we must understand the personality of its leader.

Al-Baghdadi's danger is in his elusiveness. Even though he is a powerful terrorist leader, he is not very well known. Little information can actually be confirmed about him, but he was apparently born in Iraq as Awwad Ibrahim Ali Muhammad al-Badri al-Samarrai. Most observers agree that he is a disciplined military strategist, a lucid entrepreneur, a genius recruiter, and, above all, a ruthless, cold-blooded killer. Al-Baghdadi obtained his doctorate at Iraqi University in Baghdad, which is why one of his many titles is "Doctor."[10] He is well-educated and, at one time, was an Islamic preacher. Al-Baghdadi is not a man who enjoys being in front of the camera. As a result, there are only a few pictures of him. The image that was released in January 2014 by the Iraqi government to identify him is merely a photo of a black-and-white photo.

Another reason that al-Baghdadi is so dangerous is that he is thought to be a direct descendant of the prophet Muhammad.[11] Few followers would argue that al-Baghdadi has not earned his top leadership position with ISIS; and, being considered to be in the lineage of Muhammad—whether true or not—adds to the power of his position.

It has been speculated that al-Baghdadi's stay at Camp Bucca might actually have contributed to his radicalization. Like the prisoners at Abu Ghraib, al-Baghdadi was subjected to mental and physical torment and humiliation. Reliable sources say that he spent four years in Camp Bucca, from 2005 to 2009; others say he spent only ten months in prison in 2004.[12] Colonel Kenneth King, the commanding officer in charge of Camp Bucca in 2009, remembers al-Baghdadi. "While he was dangerous, he was not one of the most dangerous, at least at the time," Colonel King said in a TV interview with CNN anchor Wolf Blitzer on June 16, 2014.[13]

In 2009, the United States was making every effort to pull out of the war in Iraq. In order to do so, it had to downsize U.S. troops there, which necessitated downsizing the number of prison guards at Camp Bucca. Large numbers of prisoners had to be set free. In 2009, the United States unwittingly released al-Baghdadi, unaware that it would encounter him again. Some confusion has arisen from the claim that al-Baghdadi was released in 2004 and therefore was not actually in prison in 2009; however, Colonel King and other guards, including James Skylar Gerrond, remember seeing al-Baghdadi in prison.[14]

Colonel King also remembers the ISIS leader saying, when he was released from prison, "I'll see you in New York."[15] And now an ISIS spokesman has pledged to raise the black flag of jihad over the White House.[16]

It is clear that al-Baghdadi intends to finish what al-Qaeda started in New York. The fantasy that ISIS will remain confined to Iraq and Syria must be dispelled, because, unfortunately, al-Baghdadi seems to be a man of his word.

Al-Qaeda in Iraq (AQI)

Soon after his release, al-Baghdad joined the fighting efforts of a group known as al-Qaeda in Iraq (AQI). It is important to note that al-Qaeda didn't necessarily start many of the groups that have fought together under its umbrella. Al-Qaeda in Iraq, which eventually morphed into ISIS, was a small group that shared the vision and purpose of al-Qaeda, and submitted, for the most part, to its leadership. This does not necessarily mean that the al-Qaeda leadership communicated directly with al-Qaeda in Iraq or ISIS. There is ample evidence that contributes to the theory that AQI/ISIS had independent leadership that was isolated from Pakistani and Afghani operations and did not adhere to the tactics and commands of the al-Qaeda leaders.

In 2010, after several leaders of al-Qaeda in Iraq were killed and jihadist morale was low, al-Baghdadi assumed leadership of the group.[17] At this time, the joint military efforts of the foreign coalition that had begun a few years earlier were paying off. Terrorist leaders were being taken out one by one, making the life expectancy of a leader like al-Baghdadi fairly short; yet his resilience, his ability to survive, and his capacity to produce results began to pay off.

Unlike former terrorist leaders, al-Baghdadi was able to learn from military skirmishes with the foreign coalition, and he adjusted his strategy accordingly. He maximized the few resources he had and used his local knowledge of Iraq to his advantage. He observed the weaknesses in the Iraqi Army and exploited their unhealthy dependence on U.S. troops. It was not long before others began to hear about al-Baghdadi's successes.

Al-Baghdadi might have been confined to Iraqi tit-for-tat battles had it not been for a change in Middle Eastern politics. Only a few months after al-Baghdadi had assumed leadership of al-Qaeda in Iraq, the uprisings known as the "Arab Spring" swept through various Middle Eastern countries.[18] Though media outlets called it a freedom movement, the Arab Spring actually contributed to the radicalization of moderate Islamic countries.

The methods and violence of ISIS plant fear in the hearts of millions of people, and much of that fear comes from a lack of understanding of what ISIS is and what it is capable of. To more fully understand the organization and its position of power today, it is essential to comprehend how the Arab Spring contributed to its success. In the following chapter, we will look at that movement in more depth.

TWO

The Arab Spring

On January 11, 2011, only a few months after al-Baghdadi came to power in Iraq, I arrived in Cairo, Egypt, to register a company that would allow Chinese missionaries in the Back to Jerusalem movement to live in the country. At the time, there were already twenty Chinese missionaries living in Cairo to plant churches in Egypt. The Chinese missionary community was growing in Cairo, and their efforts were paying off.

I hired a lawyer to help me through the process of registering a trade company that could provide both visas and jobs for the Chinese missionaries. A few days later, as we were processing the paperwork, I could see that there was discontent among the local population. Small protests were starting to pop up and block traffic, making it difficult to navigate the city by car.

Soon after I boarded a flight from Cairo to Bahrain, the Egyptian leadership fell in what became known as the Arab Spring. I later reflected on how fortunate I had been to be on that flight, because, not long after I departed, many flights to and from Cairo were canceled due to the protests and the dangerous environment. The protests seemed to be completely spontaneous.

I remained in daily contact with the Chinese missionaries in Cairo. "We are not even leaving our house," said one Chinese man who was living in an apartment building not far from the city center. "We are hanging out and having meals with our Arab neighbors because none of them are able to go to work right now," he said, so happy that he had an opportunity to minister to the locals.

The International Community Supports ISIS

However, any idea that the protests were completely spontaneous was thrown out the window when, in the middle of Arab Spring, the *New York Times* released an article that revealed the existence of a secret United States Presidential Study Directive (PSD-11) in 2010, ordering an assessment of the Muslim Brotherhood—the group that had launched the protests in Cairo in January 2011. This article suggested that President Obama supported the Muslim Brotherhood. Presidential Study Directives are usually made available on the Homeland Security Library government Web site, but PSD-11 was classified and, therefore, not made available to the public.[19]

Emboldened by the fall of the Egyptian government in February 2011, the Libyan Muslim Brotherhood (LMB) went after the leader of Libya, Muammar Gaddafi, who had relentlessly pursued the brotherhood. It was revenge time; but, this time, the LMB had support from the oddest of places. The international community backed the Muslim Brotherhood in Libya with military power to overthrow the much-hated Gaddafi. On June 9, 2011, Italy, France, Australia, Turkey, and some Middle Eastern countries pledged more than one billion U.S. dollars to aid the rebels, which were led by the Muslim Brotherhood.[20]

This international campaign to remove Muammar Gaddafi was swift and effective. Oddly, the rebel force leader whom NATO supported, Abdul-Hakim al-Hasadi, was also a former U.S. POW and a friend of Osama bin Laden. He recruited fighters from al-Qaeda in Afghanistan who had gained experience fighting U.S. soldiers.[21] In plain English, NATO financially supported known terrorists.

The fall of the Libyan government created a domino effect of fallen governments. Syria was in the rebels' sights as the next target.

Al-Baghdadi saw the mass confusion from the rise of the Muslim Brotherhood and the fall of liberal moderate Muslims as an opportunity to implement Sharia law, a rigid legal system based upon the Koran and the teachings of the prophet Muhammad.

The Rat Line

A power vacuum in the Middle East allowed jihadists to focus on a plan to attack the Syrian government, initiating the secret conveyance of jihadists and weapons to Syria.

In a clandestine operation that is still controversial today, weapons began to be transported from Benghazi, Libya (the headquarters of the Muslim Brotherhood), to Syria via Turkey. Benghazi was also where the United States had sent Ambassador John Christopher Stevens in 2011 and established a CIA annex.[22] In 2012, Ambassador Stevens and three other Americans were killed in an attack on the U.S. consulate in Benghazi. Consider the United Nations Security Council's report regarding the activities in Benghazi in March 2013:

> 168. The Syrian Arab Republic has presented a prominent destination for Libyan fighters. A number of them have joined brigades as individuals or through networks to support the Syrian opposition. While it is not the mandate of the Panel to analyse the movements of combatants

> outside Libya, military materiel has also been sent out from Libya to the Syrian Arab Republic through networks and routes passing through either Turkey or northern Lebanon.
>
> 169. Since the Panel was unable to visit the Syrian Arab Republic, much of the analysis in the present section is based on information shared by international security agencies, including those of Member States from the region, and other international sources on the ground, in addition to Libyan fighters in the Syrian Arab Republic. The Panel also completed an analysis of arms shipments seized on their way to the Syrian Arab Republic.
>
> 170. Transfers of military materiel have been organized from various locations in Libya, including Misrata and Benghazi.[23]

So, the materials, training, and money that the West had sent to support the Muslim Brotherhood rebel movement in Libya was used to support the attacks on Syria, and jihadists were there to benefit from it.

Pulitzer Prize-winner Seymour Hersh reported that the route by which the materials traveled has been called the "rat line," purportedly a CIA-organized supply chain running from Benghazi to Syria via southern Turkey.[24]

According to the United Nation's Human Development Index, prior to the Arab Spring, both Egypt and Libya had two of the highest standards of living. One of the main reasons I had traveled to Egypt to start a company was due to the long stability the country had enjoyed. Now, after the Arab Spring, both Egypt and Libya are in shambles, and the international community has moved on, focusing its eyes on Syria and leaving much wreckage and poverty in its wake. Either the international community thought it would have better luck in Syria, or it collaborated behind the scenes to support the jihadists' movement; either way, its support was in ISIS's favor.

Again, Al-Baghdadi observed the rise of the Arab Spring, the support of the international community for both the Muslim Brotherhood and al-Qaeda agents, and the fall of moderate Muslim governments; and his timing in becoming the leader of al-Qaeda in Iraq could not have been better.

The Backing of Moderate Rebels

The world community began to play an active role in the overthrow of Syrian President Bashar al-Assad by supporting "moderate" rebels. Most people who watched the Syrian events on the news at home had no clue what the term *moderate* meant in this regard. In Syria, there was no real distinction between moderate rebels and radical jihadists. There were no color-coded uniforms that identified one from the other. The word simply had no clear meaning. The term was used, however, to give Westerners a sense that they were on the side of the good guys; in truth, there were no good guys to side with.

Then, the world watched in horror as the moderate rebels whom they had been supporting attacked some of the oldest Christian communities that still speak Aramaic, the language that Jesus most likely spoke. These Christian communities had lived in peace beside Muslim societies for generations. Now, many Christians were being killed. The moderate rebels stormed into churches, tore down crosses, killed clergy members, and, in some cases, donned the robes of priests and posed for pictures.

Many young Christians were crucified, hung on crosses in public squares in Syria. Two young Christian teenagers were crucified in Damascus; one was crucified in front of his father who was afterward killed, as reported by Sister Raghida, former head nun at a Christian school in Damascus, who had witnessed the atrocity.[25] Christians were killed in other gruesome manners, as well. Sister Raghida told stories of pregnant women who were brutally attacked, and whose babies were ripped from them and hung from trees by their umbilical cords. There are video clips from the Internet of Muslims playing soccer with the heads of Christians.[26]

There is another horrific and sad video of a Christian who was forced to his knees with his hands tied behind his back in the middle of a crowd of jihadists. He was forced to renounce his faith in Jesus Christ and was promised life if he converted. "I testify that there is no god but Allah, and Muhammad is the messenger of Allah," he said to please his captors. After he renounced his faith, his Muslim captor killed him anyway by cutting off his head.[27]

Before long, the Western community discovered that the moderate rebels they had been supporting were actually radical jihadists, and, tragically, that they had been financially backing the persecution.

Foreigners Join the ISIS Military

According to the intelligence consultancy The Soufan Group, al-Baghdadi was able to enlist 12,000 militant Islamists, including 3,000 from Western countries, to join his efforts in jihad.[28] Today, the CIA estimates that al-Baghdadi could have as many as 31,500 fighters.[29] Fighters came from far and wide to join forces with al-Baghdadi, not because they were enticed by the leader's charisma, but because they believed in the cause he was fighting for.

What was it that compelled so many young Europeans to board planes and join the fight alongside al-Baghdadi? Why did so many young men leave their comfortable lives in Australia to be trained in the hot desert sands of the Middle East?

The vision of obtaining an Islamic State motivated these legions of fighters and beckoned the Islamic zealots. Al-Baghdadi inspired his followers, giving them a vision of overthrowing governments that did not abide by Sharia law.

Al-Baghdadi sold his followers the idea of establishing a caliphate. He recruited them by broadcasting the persecution of Muslims around the world and then convincing them of their duty and responsibility to repel those atrocities.

He inspired his followers through the imagery of video and of lyrical verses from the Koran. He whipped up unbridled anger in young men who were filled with more testosterone and passion than with sense. The army that he has raised is unified in anger and hatred; and its volcano of emotion is erupting over Syria, as seen in the savage acts the terrorists carry out against innocent women and children. And ISIS's atrocities and war crimes have only been made worse by the ignorance and apathy of the world community.

ISIS or ISIL?

If the situation surrounding ISIS seems perplexing to you, don't worry—you are not alone. Remember, the world's best intelligence communities have been confused by the nature and success of this terror organization, and their confusion has contributed to their befuddling responses to it. John O. Brennan, former chief counterterrorism advisor to President Obama and current director of the CIA, once dismissed the danger of ISIS and its plan to establish a caliphate. In an interview on June 29, 2011, he said,

> Our strategy is...shaped by a deeper understanding of al Qaeda's goals, strategy and tactics....I'm not talking about al Qaeda's grandiose vision of global domination through a violent Islamic caliphate. That vision is absurd, and we are not going to organize our counterterrorism policies

> against a feckless delusion that is never going to happen. We are not going to elevate these thugs and their murderous aspirations into something larger than they are.[30]

Two years after Brennan made that statement, ISIS established a caliphate in Syria and Iraq, exactly as they had said they would. The future director of the CIA never expected the "feckless delusion" to come to pass.

Few people are able to capture the general confusion that prevails among the public with regard to ISIS, but Aubrey Bailey from Fleet, Hampshire, England, who sent the following letter to the *Daily Mail* in September 2014, did a wonderful job of it.

> Are you confused by what is going on in the Middle East? Let me explain.
>
> We support the Iraqi government in the fight against Islamic State. We don't like IS, but IS is supported by Saudi Arabia, whom we do like.
>
> We don't like President Assad in Syria. We support the fight against him, but not IS, which is also fighting against him.
>
> We don't like Iran, but Iran supports the Iraqi government against IS. So, some of our friends support our enemies and some of our enemies are our friends, and some of our enemies are fighting against our other enemies, whom we want to lose, but we don't want our enemies who are fighting our enemies to win.
>
> If the people we want to defeat are defeated, they might be replaced by people we like even less. And all this was started by us invading a country to drive out terrorists who weren't actually there until we went in to drive them out. Do you understand now?[31]

The vision of ISIS is to rid both Syria and Iraq of liberal or polluted forms of Islam and to replace them with a stricter orthodoxy—Sharia law, which is based on Koranic and Muhammadan teachings.

Another acronym for the Islamic State is ISIL. ISIL stands for the Islamic State of Iraq and the Levant—a term for the countries that border the Eastern Mediterranean, including Cyprus, Jordan, Lebanon, Palestine, Turkey, and, most important, Israel. ISIL embodies a larger territory than ISIS, which is confined to Syria and Iraq.

Sometimes, ISIS and ISIL are simply called "IS," or "Islamic State." This is the most frightening of all the names, because it implies that the terrorist ambition is not limited to Syria, Iraq, or the Levant but extends to the rest of the world.

It would be a mistake to think that IS refers simply to countries run by Muslims. Malaysia and Turkey are Islamic countries, but their governmental framework is not what ISIS (ISIL, IS) has in mind. ISIS envisions an entire world under the control of one leader—the caliph.

For the purpose of clarity, and to eliminate as much confusion as possible, I will continue to use the original acronym ISIS, though it is important to note that IS is the most common expression used by the group today, because, as we've noted, their vision encompasses absolute control and a universal caliphate.

Sadly, most people do not understand the term *caliphate*; but they need to understand it if they want to understand ISIS, because everything that ISIS does revolves around the idea of a universal caliphate. Ever since the death of Muhammad, radical Muslims have envisioned a universal community in which all tribes and nations are brought under the submission of an Islamic leader.

Caliph is the name given to an Islamic leader who unites and leads the Muslim community in the way that Muhammad did. For a better understanding of this role, there is a 1,400-year caliphate history that can be reviewed. Muslims believe that Allah is in heaven and cannot personally lead his followers, so he uses caliphs to look after his interests on earth.

Because there are still so many nations today that do not submit to Islam, radical Muslims believe that they have a religious duty to arrange for an army and to call for jihad to force other religious groups and unbelievers to choose one of the three options described earlier: convert to Islam, pay *jizya*, or die. A caliphate can unite Muslim nations to fight against the infidels. As long as there are nations, or people groups, that do not submit to Allah, there will be no peace in the Islamic heart.

It should be noted that the caliphate is not the equivalent of the modern papacy at the Vatican in Rome. A caliph is not only a supreme religious leader but also a supreme military and political leader, just as Muhammad was. Additionally, in order to be a caliph, a person must be able to trace his lineage directly to Muhammad.

ISIS, Hamas, the Taliban, and al-Qaeda all have the same vision: to establish a world that is dominated by Islam. Their plan to accomplish this is to kill every Christian, Jew, and unbeliever who stands in their way. Indeed, even Muslims are not immune if they disagree with the jihadists.

The primary goal of the caliph is to capture the crown jewel—Jerusalem. Israel is located in the Levant. In recent history, Muslims have been able to conquer and occupy almost every country in the Middle East; but, for reasons that cannot be fully understood, the tiny country of Israel has defied the odds. Even though it is completely surrounded by Muslim countries, it has been able to resist and repel every attack of its Muslim neighbors.

There is no shortage of Muslim young men who are ready to fight and to die for a caliph that represents Muhammad. Many young men are ready to strap explosives to their bodies, believing that they will be blessed in the afterlife for their sacrifice in jihad against the infidel.

In June 2014, a true Islamic State had what it needed to establish a caliphate. Most important, it had a caliph, believed to be from the lineage of Muhammad, who would lead Muslims to retake the territory that rightly belonged to them.

> On June 29, 2014—or the first of Ramadan, 1435, for those who prefer the Islamic calendar to the Gregorian—the leaders of the Islamic State of Iraq and Sham (ISIS) publicly uttered for the first time a word that means little to the average Westerner, but everything to some pious Muslims. The word is "caliph." ISIS's proclamation that day formally hacked the last two letters from its acronym (it's now just "The Islamic State") and declared Abu Bakr al Baghdadi, born Ibrahim ibn Awwad ibn Ibrahim ibn Ali ibn Muhammad al-Badri al-Samarrai, the Caliph of all Muslims and the Prince of the Believers.[32]

Both Muslims who support ISIS and those who do not support ISIS can identify with the significance of establishing a caliphate. Al-Baghdadi and his propaganda team employed terms, iconology, dates, and nostalgia that harkened back to the glory days of Islam, giving modern-day Muslims a romanticized vision of the time when Islam spread like wildfire throughout the Middle East, North Africa, the Levant, and even western Europe.

ISIS is pushing for an Islamic revival, and it thirsts for the blood of infidels, the beheading of Jews and Christians, the stoning of blasphemers, and the slavery of nonbelievers.

When outsiders watch jihadists cheering and dancing as a result of their victory over enemy soldiers whom they killed, they falsely assume that these are just mad savages who were born in war-torn countries and have never known any other way of life. That view is a mistake. Osama bin Laden was born into a wealthy Saudi Arabian family. Thousands of people from countries like England, France, Australia, and Sweden have joined ISIS, too; many of these people knew nothing of war and had access to very promising lives.

ISIS members are following the mystical belief that their actions (no matter how gruesome they seem to the typical Westerner) are honored by Allah. In fact, they believe that they are fulfilling a religious duty, and they experience a religious exhilaration that can be explained only as spiritually orgasmic when they take territory and claim victory over the enemy. Remember, to the Muslim, war is as much a religious experience as it is a physical one.

ISIS believes that, once it establishes a caliphate, Muslims who now condemn them will come to praise all of their actions. Even though there are many Muslim leaders who reject al-Baghdadi's caliphal claim (especially the Shiite leadership), ISIS believes that once the caliphate has been firmly established and ISIS is able to make further advances, it will be warmly embraced.

So, al-Baghdadi is not an uneducated savage, as many might like to paint him. Nor is he an ignorant religious fanatic running around the desert like the Tasmanian Devil from the Looney Tunes cartoons. Al-Baghdadi is an educated Muslim cleric and a student of history. These facts may point to some clues that will help us to understand both his personality and his ambitions for the future.

Al-Baghdadi is not only a student of history, but he is a slave to it; he is a fanatical purist who uses both words and iconology to point to something greater. Al-Baghdadi wants Muslims to know him as the one who fulfills the prophecies and goals of the Koran and the hadith—"the collective body of traditions relating to Muhammad and his companions,"[33] just as Christians know Jesus as the One who fulfilled Old Testament prophecies.

Not only does al-Baghdadi claim to be from the lineage of Muhammad, but he also claims that Baghdad is his hometown—hence his name, al-Baghdadi. Even his initial focus on Syria is not a mistake, as it relates to Islamic end-time prophesy.

The Bloody History of Islam

It is important to look at other caliphs in history to understand the caliphate that has been established by ISIS. It seems that, as an ardent student of Islamic history and theology, al-Baghdadi has a sentimental devotion to the Abbasid caliphs, who oversaw the golden age of Islam and ruled the Abbasid Caliphate from 750 to 1258 AD. Baghdad, which is located between the Tigris and the Euphrates Rivers, only fifty miles from the ancient ruins of Babylon, was the capital of the Abbasid Caliphate, which was one of the most influential Islamic dynasties.[34]

The Abbasid Caliphate became the largest empire in the world after conquering many countries from the Atlantic to India and China and forcing the people to accept Islam. More important is how the Abbasid Caliphate was established.

Western news outlets have interviewed many scholars and Middle Eastern analysts who argue that al-Baghdadi is not a legitimate caliph, because, according to law and custom, a caliph must be elected by the majority of leading elders. Assuming command based solely on one's bloodline is more of a Shia concept. However, the Abbasid caliphs were not elected by the Syrian-based Islamic rulers, who were overthrown. The historical record shows that a caliph does not *have* to be elected by a group of Islamic elders. If that were the case, the Abbasid caliphs never would have come to power.

Westerners are too used to democratic elections and Judeo-Christian ideas of fairness, so they work hard to fit Islam into that framework, claiming that Islam is a peaceful religion. But the violence and damages inflicted by ISIS and other terrorist organizations that identify with Islam suggest otherwise.

Farid Senzai, assistant professor of politics of the Middle East at Santa Clara University, California, stated that al-Baghdadi is not supported by mainstream Muslims. "The Baghdadi caliphate is rejected by most mainstream Islamists because they feel it damages their cause to establish an Islamic system through peaceful means."[35] Though this may be true, history shows that radical Muslims, who are more powerful and often more successful than mainstream Muslims, have always used force and violence to establish Islam. These means are often veiled with ideas of freeing oppressed societies.

Together with Persian Shia Muslims, the Abbasid caliphs assumed power by leading a violent revolution against the Umayyad Caliphate, which was based in Damascus, Syria. The Umayyads did not get to vote or decide on whether there should be a *different* caliph. They were taken over by force; the changeover did not come through "peaceful means."

Prior to the time of the Abbasid caliphs, the prophet Muhammad and his followers were actually kicked out of Mecca by its citizens; but Muhammad came back and established his rule there—and not by peaceful means, either.

The Umayyads did not vote for a caliph; those living in Mecca did not vote for a caliph; the Syrians did not vote for a caliph; and the people of Iraq and Iran did not vote for a caliph—none of these areas were conquered peacefully.

Claiming that al-Baghdadi cannot be caliph because of his violent methods of establishing his power—which ruins PR campaigns—has not kept him from taking leadership. In fact, his actions line up with Islamic history. ISIS is not doing anything that is out of the historical norm for Islam. To Muslims living in, for example, Stockholm today, ISIS's methods of violence and terrorism might not be normal (this may be due to their exposure to Judeo-Christian society), but ISIS is gravitating back to the historical core of Islam.

Muhammad's End-time Prophecy

Both Iraq and Syria are significant to ISIS. The war that the terrorist group is fighting in these two countries is not just for the purpose of establishing a caliphate in a random area. It goes much deeper than that. The meaning behind the conflict in Syria is even apocalyptic.

> "If you think all these mujahideen [jihadists] came from across the world to fight [Syrian President] Assad, you're mistaken," said a Sunni Muslim jihadi who uses the name Abu Omar and fights in one of the many anti-Assad Islamist brigades in Aleppo.
>
> "They are all here as promised by the Prophet. This is the war he promised—it is the Grand Battle," he told Reuters, using a word which can also be translated as slaughter.[36]

The Islamic version of Armageddon teaches that Syria will be the location of the final battle, where the blood that is shed will run knee deep through the streets. Hundreds of thousands of people will be killed. The Saudi Arabian cities of Mecca and Medina will collapse.

So, when the international community launches air strikes against ISIS, and the Muslim jihadists see bombs, destruction, and death—they are not surprised. In fact, the attacks fulfill their own prophesies and serve to encourage them. They believe that the day of final judgment will take place in Syria.

Are you starting to understand the historical events and the theological ideas that are influencing ISIS? This group is not full of freedom fighters who want independence for downtrodden people. Its members are attempting to gain absolute control, to establish a caliphate that will rule an end-time Islamic empire. ISIS's religious firebrand attains even more legitimacy when his followers are attacked in Syria, pointing to the fulfillment of Muhammad's grand end-time prophesy.

Again, none of the information given in this book is exhaustive, but, hopefully, it helps to piece together some of the bigger parts of the ISIS puzzle. ISIS is not a group of mysterious monsters that have been hiding under a bed to emerge when the lights go out. They have been around for some time and can be traced back to their roots as jihadists who were loyal to al-Qaeda.

How can we sum up the rise of al-Baghdadi? When he was a young man, the ISIS leader studied as a common cleric in university in Baghdad. As stated earlier, he was not from a prestigious, wealthy family, as was Osama bin Laden; he was just a run-of-the-mill, dedicated Muslim who lived under the rule of Saddam Hussein. After the United States invaded Iraq, he ended up in a U.S. prison, where he rubbed shoulders with some pretty bad people. After his release, he found himself on the fast track to leadership of the dying zealots group called Al-Qaeda in Iraq, until the Arab Spring opened a door to a much greater opportunity.

THREE

Brother Yun and the Back to Jerusalem Vision

In September 2014, a Chinese pastor named Brother Yun flew from Germany to Los Angeles, California. I had flown in from my home in China to meet him and to begin our "Bless Your Enemies" tour.

Brother Yun is one of the most well-known Chinese pastors in the world. The story of his life, entitled *The Heavenly Man*, has been translated into many languages, and he is one of the major voices for the "Back to Jerusalem" vision of the underground church.

Though he is a famous pastor, Brother Yun has never owned a passport. He travels by way of refugee papers issued by an EU country. Unfortunately, that day in September, he was on a flight full of Middle Eastern passengers flying into the United States by way of refugee papers, as well.

Upon their arrival in America, Brother Yun and his wife, Deling, were taken out of the immigration line and sent to a separate immigration room. They were questioned over and over by an officer who spoke German.

"They asked me so many questions about my refugee papers and why we were flying into the U.S. from Europe," Brother Yun told me when he finally it was admitted into the country.

"They kept me and my wife in the immigration office for several hours asking me questions. They were worried about our flight because it was so full of Middle Easterners with special passports and refugee papers from Europe. I could tell that they were nervous, and I assumed it was because the alert from ISIS had been so high. In German, I told them that I was a pastor and that I was coming to America to preach at churches. The officer interviewing me told me that they wanted to make sure that I was not in the country to cause problems."

As mentioned earlier, ISIS's vision is not limited to Iraq and Syria alone. It is an inspiring vision for radical Muslims around the world; consequently, it knows no boundaries.

Nevertheless, the leaders of ISIS are unaware that they are not the only ones hunting for "infidels." Missionaries from the underground church in China, represented by Brother Yun, are launching a spiritual offensive. They are not armed with a sentence of death but with the message of life, and ISIS jihadists are in their crosshairs.

Especially Qualified

How do you negotiate with people who seek absolute domination? How do you stop someone who believes that killing one's enemies is rewarded in the afterlife? Where would one start a mediation process with ISIS, when its members require the death of the infidel? Is there any hope of compromise, of finding middle ground?

We have seen that the ISIS problem poses questions that some of the most highly paid experts around the world have struggled to answer. Governments, diplomats, megacompanies, and militaries have spent billions of dollars to obtain advice and to employ strategies to stop this terrorist organization. A number of pie charts, flowcharts, and acronyms have been developed to try to deal with it, but nothing has seemed to work.

Many experts are convinced that ISIS is a political problem that requires a political answer. But what if these experts are wrong? What if ISIS is not chiefly a political problem? What if it is a spiritual one?

As stated in the preface, I write this book not from the perspective of a Middle East expert but from that of Chinese missionaries who are focused on taking the gospel to ISIS.

The challenges and demands that accompany a missionary outreach to ISIS are not entirely new to the Chinese who share the Back to Jerusalem vision. For generations, Chinese Christians have dealt with a Communist government that has vehemently opposed them. Often, that government has sought nothing less than the complete annihilation of Christianity in China, leaving absolutely no room for compromise. Like ISIS, the Communist government has demanded conversion (though, in this case, conversion to atheism) or death. At least ISIS offers a third option.

ISIS wounded or killed at least 26,000 people in 2014.[37] Although this number is truly devastating, Communist leader Mao Zedong (Tse-tung), "who for decades held absolute power over the lives of one-quarter of the world's population, was responsible for well over 70 million deaths in peacetime, more than any other twentieth-century leader."[38]

Mao Zedong killed more people than the populations of Iraq, Syria, Lebanon, and Israel put together! People have died under ISIS in gruesome ways, but let us not forget what the Chinese went through during the "Great Leap Forward," which was no less gruesome and happened on a much greater scale. Today, there is much international resistance to those perpetrating the violence in Iraq; but, when Mao Zedong was in power in China, there was absolutely no international resistance. The world averted its eyes. One reason is that, after WWII, many nations had "war fatigue." The Korean War further took away the international community's appetite for opposing what China was doing to its own people.

On October 1, 1949, Mao established his rule over China, with the backdrop of Tiananmen Square, to impose the will of the Communist Party over the country. Similarly, ISIS has made it very clear that it is Muslim, that it is establishing a caliphate, and that it will impose Sharia law on every area it controls.

The Chinese missionaries are therefore in a unique place to understand what is going on in the Middle East, particularly in regard to ISIS's oppression and its insatiable desire for absolute power and control in the form of a caliphate.

Failed Strategies with ISIS

ISIS is threatening the safety of the next generation, as well as the future of the world. The danger is increasing, and, as we have seen, the wealthiest and most powerful countries in the world do not know how to avert it. No amount of money, expertise, or diplomacy that has been employed to quell ISIS has made it go away. And the millions of dollars that have been spent on bombing campaigns do not appear to be having any long-term effect.

Moreover, the United Nations is helpless to do anything about it. Its policies of diplomacy and its empty threats have not worked. It has been merely a paper tiger in its dealings with ISIS.

There is a wry joke circulating that illustrates the forcefulness of ISIS and the ineffectiveness of the UN. The United Nations sees a meteorite coming toward the earth, so its secretary sends a message to the meteorite to warn it to change its course. But the meteorite continues on its path toward the earth. So, on behalf of the world community, the UN sends a "strongly worded" letter warning the meteorite that a failure to change its course might result in a more strongly worded letter in the future. Nevertheless, the meteorite continues its trajectory, so the UN issues a series of economic sanctions against it. When the meteorite finally crashes to earth, the UN issues a statement of tolerance and understanding toward it on behalf of all nations and makes the meteorite a member of the UN Security Council!

Not only have most of our preconceptions about ISIS been wrong, but our analyses of the terrorist group, even after some study and exposure to it, are most likely skewed, as well. A whole book could be written about everything we *don't* understand about ISIS.

Another issue is that Western nations are currently experiencing war weariness, and their leaders are grasping after ideas and strategies that they hope will achieve security. No country wants to continue putting its young men and women in harm's way in the desert sands of Iraq. We have already seen that show and do not want a repeat of it.

Many people have tried to wash their hands of both Iraq and Syria, to be finished with them, but Iraq is not a country that can be ignored or forgotten. Iraq is home to one of the oldest civilizations in the world, and it is the proud owner of much underground "black gold"—oil.

The problem of ISIS is not lessening. Iraqi Christians are still being killed and slaughtered, but Christians are not the only ones who are being threatened. Tens of thousands of Kurds and Yazidis are being attacked, raped, sold as slaves, and even killed by ISIS.

ISIS has a relatively small army; but, with superior support, fire power, and funding, it is taking on other armies—and it is winning. With a military that is maintained by a wealth of natural resources and is carrying out the commands of an Islamic cleric who believes in the absolute authority of the Koran, is anyone safe?

ISIS is not content with enjoying the success of past military conquests; it is obsessed with continued victory and with the complete and absolute annihilation of the nation of Israel. Furthermore, it will not flinch at destroying any person or nation who gets in its way.

Fighting the Wrong Fight?

For generations, the nations of the world have been waging battles in the Middle East in their own strength, and what good has it done? What about the tactic of using sanctions? Has this method worked? Since 1979, sanction after sanction has been imposed on Iran. Military plan after military plan has been employed in the region, but is the situation there any better? Really, has anything changed? Is Iran intimidated by these efforts? Have its nuclear ambitions been abandoned?

Similarly, since the 1950s, thousands of peacekeeping troops have been stationed on the border of North Korea to contain that nation from endangering its neighbors and the rest of the world. Yet is North Korea any less of a threat today than it was sixty years ago?

ISIS has been bombed in military campaigns year after year, and some of its leaders have been thrown into prison. Is ISIS any less dangerous?

Iraqis are running away from ISIS in terror, and many are being killed. Iraq was set free by a "coalition of the willing" in 2003; but from what were they freed? Saddam Hussein? Saddam was no choirboy, but was he worse than ISIS?

Could it be that we have been fighting the wrong fight? As the Bible says, *"we do not wrestle against flesh and blood, but against the rulers, against the authorities, against the cosmic powers over this present darkness"* (Ephesians 6:12).

A New Approach to ISIS

The world has tried numerous methods in its attempts to stop ISIS. After an expenditure of billions of dollars, and after consulting many experts and military specialists, maybe we need to try a different strategy. There is another approach that has yet to be explored and employed. It is one that Jesus taught in the Sermon on the Mount:

> *You have heard that it was said, "You shall love your neighbor and hate your enemy." But I say to you, Love your enemies and pray for those who persecute you, so that you may be sons of your Father who is in heaven.* (Matthew 5:43–45)

What if, contrary to previous techniques, we employed the strategy of Jesus when dealing with the enemies of Christianity? What if we *love our enemies?*

"Foolish!" "Impossible!" "Naive!" "Suicidal!" people will say.

Yet think about what might happen if, instead of dropping bombs, we distributed Bibles? If, instead of deploying soldiers, we sent missionaries? If, instead of pursuing war, we sought to send the best gift of love that has ever been given to mankind?

Back to Jerusalem missionaries from China are doing exactly that! They are traveling from the most rural areas of China to Syria and to the mountains of northern Iraq. The goal of the Chinese underground house church is to launch this alternative type of "offensive" against ISIS.

Believers in the underground church are not fighting ISIS; rather, they are joining their brothers and sisters on the other side of the "enemy lines." ISIS is not the enemy; it is only an instrument being used for evil by our true enemy—Satan. We must recognize the difference. We do not fight against flesh and blood.

Let me clarify that blessing one's enemies should not be confused with modern views of pacifism. Nor should it be confused with appeasement, which is the opposite of love. Appeasement is, essentially, self-preservation prompted by fear. In contrast, true love focuses on the preservation of others, even at the expense of oneself; and it certainly does not mean that there will be no fierce opposition and confrontation.

Imagining that one might appease ISIS in order to secure safety for oneself is a sad illusion. However, making an honest effort toward diplomacy and dialogue between Muslims and Christians may promote understanding. A true invasion of love will inevitably meet the most violent protectors of the Islamic stronghold.

Muslim leadership does not want truth (or the Truth), because the truth will free the slaves who have been held captive for generations. (See John 8:31–32.) In order to maintain control, the enemy must use its tools to preserve an atmosphere of both ignorance and fear. Radical Islam sadly promotes both of these tools—but love can defeat them.

Catalysts for Transformation

Let us step back and evaluate the idea of sending missionaries to Iraq. Is it naive to believe that a well-meaning, unarmed, "bleeding-heart" Chinese missionary with a Bible could really make a difference among the members of ISIS? Is it nothing more than senseless suicide to embark on such a mission?

Maybe not. Perhaps missionaries are actually change agents who can impact societies more than has ever been realized. Recent groundbreaking research shows that many elements found in free and healthy societies are, at their origin, linked to the presence of missionaries. This new evidence might actually shed light on why, if the dark heart of Islam is not addressed, democracy and free markets will not work in the Middle East.

Robert Woodberry, a sociologist and an associate professor at the National University of Singapore, has conducted numerous studies on the role of missionaries throughout history, and he has found that many of them have been pivotal catalysts in transforming societies for the better.

Woodberry's research gives conclusive evidence that, over the last three hundred years, missionaries have been among the most significant factors in creating healthy, free societies. According to Woodberry's research,

> Areas where Protestant missionaries had a significant presence in the past are on average more economically developed today, with comparatively better health, lower infant mortality, lower corruption, greater literacy, higher educational attainment (especially for women), and more robust membership in nongovernmental associations.[39]

If missionaries have been making societies better for hundreds of years, wouldn't their presence in areas controlled by ISIS likewise cause transformation? What makes us think that missionaries must wait for diplomatic channels to make life better for oppressed peoples before they can truly start to work? What if it were the other way around?

Woodberry's findings are already sending shock waves throughout the world of academia. If his conclusions are correct, then the work of missionaries not only yields the salvation of lost souls but also is one of the single largest contributors to the health of nations, benefitting generation after generation.

In 2009, *Al Jazeera* (English edition) ran a report about U.S. soldiers violating rules by handing out Bibles. This distribution was not organized by the military but was initiated by individuals who served in the U.S. military, because they could see such a huge need for them.

Sergeant Jon Watt, one of those interviewed for the report, said, "I bought a carpet and then I gave the guy a Bible after I conducted my business…The expressions that I got from the people in Iraq [were] just phenomenal, they were hungry for The Word."[40]

Al Jazeera published that report on May 4. The following day, Army spokeswoman Major Jennifer Willis told Reuters that the Bibles were collected and burned.[41] The Bibles were not the property of the United States military. Yet they were not collected and sent back to the church that donated them. They were burned.

Bombs were dropped, and Bibles were burned. But what if Bibles had been "dropped" on the enemy, and the bombs had been destroyed? Would the results have been any worse than the crisis we are dealing with today?

The people living in countries without God's Word are in darkness and desperately need the light of Christ. Sending in troops and bombing the population is a bit like punishing the victim. "You did not get to choose where you were born," Brother Yun preached at a small Mennonite church in Brooklyn, New York, on October 6, 2014. "You did not get to choose who your parents would be or what the color of your skin would be. You were not given an option."

Likewise, the people of Iraq did not choose to be born into the darkness of Islam. But there is this promise in the Bible: "*Whosoever shall call upon the name of the Lord shall be saved*" (Romans 10:13). And what words come after that promise?

How then shall they call on him in whom they have not believed? And how shall they believe in him of whom they have not heard? And how shall they hear without a preacher? And how shall they preach, except they be sent?

(Romans 10:14–15 KJV)

The Difference Between Western Europe and the Middle East

Essentially, Western Europeans are not freer because they have a superior form of government. They are not wealthier because they have stolen from poor countries, and they do not have a more efficient free market. They are certainly not smarter or more hard-working than the Iraqis and Syrians who are fighting for ISIS.

The difference between Western Europe and the Middle East is in the missionary.

The message that is carried by a Christian missionary—the good news of Jesus Christ—is water to the thirsty, food to the hungry, freedom to the enslaved, power to the downtrodden, justice to the persecuted, enlightenment to the ignorant, hope for the hopeless, and the only message that gives life to those facing death by ISIS.

Jonah's message to the Ninevites was only as powerful as their willingness to receive it. (See Jonah 3.) North Korea and South Korea are a modern illustration of that truth. They share similar histories, cultures, and languages. Yet, although they occupy the same isolated peninsula, the two countries could not be more different.

North Korean government officials have embraced and enforced atheism, and they have clung to the theory of evolution as the building block of human history. They have persecuted and killed Christians and have destroyed churches and Christian literature. They continue to be one of the most abusive governments in the world, and they target believers in Jesus Christ.

In South Korea, Christians enjoy freedom and protection. Regular envoys of South Koreans even travel to Israel to show support and solidarity with the Jewish people. Science, medicine, business, and even leisure activities flourish in South Korea. In contrast, in North Korea, education and recreation have withered and are on life support.

We could similarly contrast the acceptance of Christianity in West Germany versus its rejection in East Germany; or the periods of relative freedom for Christians in China as opposed to the periods of intense persecution of Christians there. Moreover, in Russia, the times of systematic persecution versus national support for Christians might even be said to be linked to the relative length of its soup lines.

God said to Abraham,

> *And I will make of thee a great nation, and I will bless thee, and make thy name great; and thou shalt be a blessing: and I will bless them that bless thee, and curse him that curseth thee: and in thee shall all families of the earth be blessed.*
>
> (Genesis 12:2–3 KJV)

Back to Jerusalem missionaries from China have seen first-hand what God's truth can do in their nation. They know what it is like to suffer in darkness and what it takes to change the trajectory of a nation that persecutes Christians. The growing number of believers in China, in spite of a historical past riddled with persecution, is directly connected to the economic, political, and social freedoms that they currently enjoy.

We Won't Win the Battle "Standing Up"

Since the ISIS problem is political rather than spiritual, it is impossible to win the battle against ISIS standing up. As Christians, we must drop to our knees in prayer and allow God to move in people's hearts. Members of ISIS cannot be saved by bullets and bombs. There are not enough soldiers in the world to correct the problem or to protect the world from the growing threat. Fighting ISIS with military strength alone will only exacerbate the situation.

Al-Baghdadi models himself after Muhammad, and ISIS's ideology is driven by the teachings of the Koran. The Koran cannot be overcome by a secular government; it can be superseded only by the power of Jesus Christ.

Therefore, the only rational way to "beat" ISIS is to send in missionaries whose ideologies are based on the Bible. The missionaries who fight this battle must model themselves after Jesus Christ, not Muhammad. The missionaries who go to the Middle East to target ISIS must have the Word of God as a primary weapon in their arsenal, and they must love their enemies and be ready to sacrifice their lives for them.

FOUR

The Five W's of Islam

Many honest Christians listen to the opinions of some of the world's most respected leaders who claim that Islam is a peaceful religion that has been hijacked by a fringe group of fanatics. These Christians ask themselves if the violence carried out by other fringe groups in the name of Jesus is similar to that which is carried out by ISIS in the name of Muhammad. If the words of Jesus can be twisted to fit the motives of terrorists, why is it not a stretch to believe that the same can be done by Islamic fringe groups in the name of Muhammad? The answer to this question is of the utmost importance for understanding ISIS.

The knowledge that most of us have about Islam comes purely through impressions we receive from media reports and interviews, or perhaps from personal observation. We have not tapped into Koranic teachings, theologically dissected the Hadith, or thoroughly researched Muhammad's life. Few non-Muslims sit down and study Islamic history.

Most people reflect on what they have personally observed, and they base their conclusions on those observations. That is essentially the method that you and I use when we discuss various issues with our family members or friends over coffee in our own homes.

The things that we have observed about Islam on the news may seem pretty straightforward. The Pew Research Center conducted a poll in September 2014 that showed that many Americans—from young to old, liberal to conservative—were concerned about the rise of Islamic extremism in the last three years.[42] Why was there such a dramatic rise of concern about Islamic extremism? Because Americans have observed, through the news media and on social media, the killing of innocent people by ISIS. We have observed this terrorist group ruthlessly killing people in the name of Islam.

But is this perspective too simplistic?

Evaluating Islam

This chapter is not the only one in which we will evaluate the merits of Islam. We will examine Islam and Islamic teachings throughout this book, because it is impossible to separate ISIS from Islam. However, for now, it seems appropriate to evaluate the religion that is behind ISIS but is separate from it. It may not be possible to evaluate ISIS without looking at Islam, but it is certainly possible to evaluate Islam without looking at ISIS. ISIS is relatively new; Islam has been around for well over a thousand years.

The volumes of books that have been written about Islam—both for it and against it—could drain an ocean of ink. People have sacrificed and devoted their lives to make the truth about Islam known. However, the average person would never pick up one of those volumes, let alone make a concerted effort to learn about Islam.

To give you an overview of the impact of Islam in the world, and to aid you in remembering this information, we will look at five main categories in relation to it. If you remember these basic categories, you will be able to help others understand why Islam is so influential. In any debate or conversation on Islam, I guarantee that one or more of the following topics will be mentioned.

The categories are arranged under what I call "the five *w*'s"—the who, what, when, where, and why—of Islam. I am not using the five *w*'s in the usual context, as would a reporter, a student, or my fifth grade teacher (who most likely would be appalled by my use of it); I am using it as an acronym to help you understand the basics of Islam.

Here, then, are the five *w*'s of Islam:

- *Who* was the prophet Muhammad?
- *What* is the Koran and what does it teach?
- *When* was Islam established?
- *Where* do the majority of Muslims live?
- *Why* Islam?

If you learn the answers to these five questions as you evaluate Islam, you may come to a very unpleasant conclusion, which may not make you very popular at parties or political fund-raising events.

Thomas Jefferson once said, "Honesty is the first chapter in the book of wisdom."

If groups that use violence in the name of Islam do not represent the true nature of Islam, then that should be easy to prove. The five *w*'s, in order, are successive and build from the foundation of the prophet, or the founder, of the religion—Muhammad.

1. Who Was the Prophet Muhammad?

The prophet Muhammad is the cornerstone of Islam, which was built on the revelations given to him. Just as Abraham is the father of Judaism (ergo, Father Abraham), and Jesus is the genesis of Christianity, so, too, the prophet Muhammad is the father of Islam. So, we will begin with an evaluation of the Islamic founder to help us understand Islam. It is not my intent to insult or slander the prophet Muhammad or to offend any Muslim believer. Muslims are my brothers and sisters, and it is my hope that we can show the love and goodness of God to them.

Muhammad is regarded as the last prophet. All the teachings and holy writings in Islam, including the Koran, are derived from his actions, teachings, and revelations.

Some suggest that, to understand Islam, studying the Koran and learning Arabic are not as essential as studying the prophet Muhammad. I agree, and therefore I will spend more time discussing Muhammad than the other subjects.

Muhammad is one of the more controversial figures in history. In 2005, a seemingly simple, harmless Danish newspaper published cartoons that depicted the image of the prophet Muhammad, an act that is strictly forbidden in Islam. Few people have ever dared to depict the image of Muhammad, in fear of offending Muslims; but the Danish journalists apparently assumed that they lived in a more tolerant time in Europe. They were wrong.

Worldwide protests erupted, embassies were attacked, sanctions were enacted, Danish diplomats were kicked out of Arab countries, and roughly 250 people were killed and 800 injured.[43]

In Islam, Muhammad is so central that the Koran commands Muslims to obey Muhammad and follow him just as they would obey and follow their god, Allah. (See Koran 4:59.)

According to the Koran, Muhammad is the perfect example of how Muslim men should behave. (See Koran 33:21.) If anyone criticizes Muhammad, he is considered to be offensive to Allah, the Koran, and all Muslims.

The three main sources used by Muslims to learn more about Muhammad are the Koran, the Hadith, and Sīrat Rasūl Allāh, or just Al-sīra, which are terms for traditional biographies of the prophet Muhammad's life; what is found in these three Islamic sources should be a cause of great concern for anyone anticipating peace in Islam. The more that these three sources are made available online and studied, the more Muslim resistance we can anticipate, because these sources contradict the claim that Islam is a religion of peace.

According to Islamic writings, when the prophet Muhammad received his revelations from Allah's archangel Gabriel, he made many attempts to lead the Christians, the Jews, and the polytheists in Mecca to his version of monotheism. He was mostly mocked and rejected. The claim of Islam as being a religion of peace originates from this time period.

After much effort, Muhammad's converts consisted of his wife, his slaves, and some disenfranchised foreigners. His continued call for monotheism was bad for business in Mecca, which needed polytheistic visitors to support its economy. Even the tribe that Muhammad was born into, the Quraysh, grew increasingly agitated with him. The Quraysh, thought to be descendants of Ishmael, had a lucrative business as the keepers of the Ka'aba, a temple in Mecca with 360 idols, which was the object of many religious pilgrimages.

The Ka'aba, a former pagan temple, is now the most important structure in Islam, which is why Muslims face it when they pray. It contains the holy Black Stone of Mecca, which, oddly, is enshrined in a silver frame that resembles female genitalia, giving credence to the theory that it was a pagan object of worship prior to Islam.

Every year, millions of Muslims travel to the Ka'aba, a pilgrimage known as the "Hajj." Some Muslims spend their entire life savings to make the trip, coincidently carrying on the legacy of the journeys, with their economic boon to Mecca, that the Quraysh benefitted from so many years ago.

Muhammad primarily shared his revelations by word of mouth, since he was illiterate; but after being rejected and persecuted, he fled Mecca and found refuge under the protection of Christians in Ethiopia.[44] Eventually, when Muhammad received a revelation that three ancient goddesses inside the Ka'aba were deities (see Koran 53:19–20), along with Allah, he returned to Mecca. The Meccans were delighted that Muhammad had recognized their goddesses, and they welcomed him warmly.

However, this harmony was short-lived; Muhammad admitted that the revelation he had been given was from Satan, and, consequently, what became known as the "Satanic Verses" in the Koran were removed from the book. Muhammad fled for his life to Medina, where he found refuge and created an Islamic charter uniting the tribes of Medina, including Jews and Christians.

But Muhammad needed financing. He would not be able to establish a movement without funds. So, seeing the caravans that passed by as a source of revenue, he perfected the art of raiding. Conveniently, Muhammad received revelation that Muslims were permitted to fight and to take from others, because they had been wronged. (See Koran 22:39.) Essentially, he became a pirate with religious convictions and led a band of robbers.

> Whenever he planned a raid he would go to the mosque and gather any and all around him who might be interested in participating. He would answer questions and then select his raiding party from among the volunteers.[45]

This approach shows two things. First, if Muhammad was a prophet establishing a religion of peace, he was going about it the wrong way. Second, the mosque that Muhammad had established in Medina appeared to be a better place to recruit marauders than the local watering hole.

> [Muhammad] was a truly great general. In the space of a single decade he fought eight major battles, led eighteen raids, and planned another thirty-eight military operations where others were in command but operating under his orders and strategic direction.[46]

Having succeeded in robbing caravans, he began launching guerrilla attacks in other areas and eventually marched on to Mecca. In Koran 8:41, Muhammad details how the booty of war should be divided up.

The members of a Jewish tribe that had double-crossed Muhammad were not given mercy when they begged for it. Instead, every male was forced to kneel down before being beheaded, much like we see ISIS doing today. An estimated 700 males were executed.[47]

In addition, Muhammad took their wives and children as bounty. Muslims do not need to show mercy to unbelievers, for, according to one command in the Koran, "Muhammad is God's apostle. Those who follow him are ruthless to the unbelievers but merciful to one another."[48]

Muhammad made it clear that, since childhood, he had not been trained to be peaceful, saying, "I have been raised for jihad and I am not raised for tillage."[49]

Muhammad did not nickname himself "al-Mahi," or "the obliterator"—as recorded in *Suhih Muslim*, one of the Hadiths in Sunni Islam—because he was a broker of peace. Muhammad is even known to have enjoyed using his weapons of battle so much that he named them.

Uqbah ibn Abi Mu'ayt, a poet who wrote unfavorably about Muhammad and who threw animal entrails at the prophet while he prayed, was ordered to be killed. "Who shall look after my family?" the poet asked in his last moments.

"Hell," Muhammad responded.

Asmā bint Marwān, the famous Medina poetess and mother of five, was also guilty of composing an unfavorable poem about Muhammad, so he ordered her death. Muhammad's assassin plunged his sword into her body while she was nursing her child. Afterward, Muhammad rewarded the assassin.

This massacre of people is exactly what ISIS is reenacting today. The above instances are enough to show the kind of example Muhammad set over a number of years. The scope of Muhammad's life of violence, pillage, rape, murder, and debauchery are too numerous for this chapter but can be independently studied.

Those who argue that Muhammad was a peaceful prophet purely on the basis of his life prior to fleeing to Medina have a serious problem. Before he fled to Medina, Muhammad was not in any position of strength to demand conformity or to wield violence. The genuineness of one's peace, mercy, and forgiveness is severely tested when one is given a position of strength, as was Muhammad. It is therefore impossible to know if Muhammad's pre-Medina words of peace and love were true words or merely part of an exercise in patience as he waited to obtain enough power to impose his ideology. We do know that when Muhammad was in a position of power, his display of peace and love was usually absent.

2. What Is the Koran, and What Does It Teach?

The Koran has been a shaping force in many parts of the world. Today, entire countries are legislated by teachings originating exclusively from Muhammad and the Koran. The ideology of ISIS is based entirely upon the Koran, though many people argue they have a skewed interpretation of it.

What Is the Koran?

As stated earlier, Muhammad is the most perfect model for Muslims, and the Koran is the word of Allah revealed to him. Unlike Muhammad, Jesus never wrote a book. He never led an army. He never killed human beings. The words that His disciples recorded were of love, peace, and forgiveness. To understand parts of the Bible that seem to contradict each other, one can look at Jesus' actions to help guide interpretation.

The same goes for Koranic teachings: To understand passages that seem to contradict each other, one can look at the example of Muhammad to help guide interpretation. This, of course, presents a very large problem for Muslims who claim that Islam is a religion of peace, because the life of Muhammad does not offer a promising context for interpreting the Koran.

The Koran is not in chronological order and, at times, is admittedly a bit incoherent. When the chapters of the Koran are arranged in chronological order, there is a clear division between Muhammad's pre-Medina life—the period prior to his persecution in Mecca and flight to Medina—and his post-Medina life—the period in which he returned to Mecca as a military conqueror. Muhammad's life during the pre-Medina period is more along the lines of what many people would call "moderate" and has more in common with Judeo-Christian values. The post-Medina period of his life contains more radical elements, which is the source of the Koranic ideology that we see exhibited today.

What Does the Koran Teach? A Comparison of the Koran and the Bible

The Koran is not completely original, as it contains many passages from the Bible that Christians would recognize. If you compare the Bible to the Koran, you may notice that the events occur in reverse order. The Bible begins with Creation, followed by the fall of humanity, the calling of Abraham, the destruction of sinful places like Sodom and Gomorrah, and the law of Moses; then it goes on to the redemption and restoration of humanity through the love, grace, and mercy of Jesus Christ. The events in the Koran, however, appear in the opposite order. If followed chronologically, concepts that can be argued as loving and merciful appear first in the Koran, followed by more intolerant teachings of law, punishment, and Sodom-and-Gomorrah-like destruction.

Some parts of the Koran have messages that teach peace, such as Koran 5:32, which is quoted most often:

> We decreed upon the Children of Israel that whoever kills a soul unless for a soul or for corruption [done] in the land—it is as if he had slain mankind entirely. And whoever saves one—it is as if he had saved mankind entirely. And our messengers had certainly come to them with clear proofs. Then indeed many of them, [even] after that, throughout the land, were transgressors.

This verse also appears in the Talmud. (See Mishnah, Sanhedrin 4:5.) However, the next verse is often omitted in debates about peace:

> Indeed, the penalty for those who wage war against Allah and His Messenger and strive upon earth [to cause] corruption is none but that they be killed or crucified or that their hands and feet be cut off from opposite sides or that they be exiled from the land. (Koran 5:33)

But there is one exception: "Except for those who return [repenting] before you apprehend them. And know that Allah is Forgiving and Merciful" (Koran 5:34). Those who convert will be shown mercy.

The Koran contains at least 109 chapters, or surahs, that call Muslims to war with nonbelievers, and 164 that relate to jihad.[50] These 164 surahs refer to violent jihad, but there are many other verses on jihad that indirectly refer to violence. Many of these 164 surahs are just as violent and graphic as Koran 5:33.

Fellow Muslims are not exempt from the violence. The common argument used by Muslims and supporters of Muslims is that Christians are also guilty of killing Muslims, as if in a type of modern crusade, but this is not supported by facts. Statistically, Muslims are much more likely to be killed by other Muslims. Daniel Pipes, director of the Middle East Forum, and Gunnar Heinsohn point out, "Some 11,000,000 Muslims have been violently killed since 1948, of which 35,000, or 0.3 percent, died during the sixty years of fighting Israel, or just 1 out of every 315 Muslim fatalities. In contrast, over 90 percent of the 11 million who perished were killed by fellow Muslims."[51]

At first glance, the violence in the Koran might seem very familiar to those who have read and studied the Old Testament. Muhammad, it could be argued, was no different from King David, who slaughtered his enemies at the command of God, or even King Saul, who was commanded to kill every man, woman, and child of the Amalekite tribe (see 1 Samuel 15:1–3); but that would be an inequitable comparison.

There are some major differences between the Koran and the Bible. One is that, unlike the violence in the Bible, the violence in the Koran is open-ended. The Koran is full of god-given, firsthand commands that are to apply to every generation. Readers of the Koran are left with a responsibility to immediately carry out its commands, regardless of time, place, or setting.

Much of the Old Testament is more of a historical account, written in relation to specific people, places, and times. The reader of the Old Testament does not walk away with the commission to kill the Amalekite tribe. The open-ended command of the Bible is to love, to forgive, and to show mercy—not to destroy and to kill.

The messages of the Koran and the Bible could not be more different. There are similarities between the Torah and the Bible. That is why many people use the term "Judeo-Christian" rather than "Judeo-Christian-Islamic." The Judeo-Christian ethos is completely different from the Islamic ethos. The values and goals laid out in the Koran are incompatible with Christianity and Judaism, unless a generous amount of cherry-picking is involved.

Koranic teachings that are often used as a bridge to Judeo-Christian ideas and concepts are temporal and subject to abrogation. The Koranic verses given to Muhammad prior to his exile to Medina can be updated or changed, which means that the early inspirations that are often recited are both subjective and subordinate to the later, post-Medina inspirations. Aside from the portion of revelation given to Muhammad from Satan (the "Satanic Verses"), other revelations can be replaced or updated by later revelations by Muhammad. This can be confusing, but the Koran says, "We do not abrogate a verse or cause it to be forgotten *except* that We bring forth [one] better than it or similar to it. Do you not know that Allah is over all things competent?" (Koran 2:106, emphasis added).

A clear example of Koranic abrogation can be seen in the often-recited Koran 2:256: "There shall be no compulsion in [acceptance of] the religion." This concept seems very compatible with both Jewish and Christian teachings but is abrogated in several different areas of the Koran, most notably in Koran 9:29:

> Fight those who do not believe in Allah or in the Last Day and who do not consider unlawful what Allah and His Messenger have made unlawful and who do not adopt the religion of truth from those who were given the Scripture—[fight] until they give the jizyah willingly while they are humbled.

Or consider Koran 8:12:

> I will cast terror into the hearts of those who disbelieved, so strike [them] upon the necks and strike from them every fingertip.

Please keep in mind that this does not mean that those who follow the Koran are evil and violent. The problem is with the ideology, not the people. However, anyone using the Koran to promote peace and harmony will have an uphill battle. There are not many positive role models in early Islamic history.

The material covered in this chapter is only a small fraction of what the Koran says and teaches. The Koran is available for free and can be read by anyone with an Internet connection.[52] I own a copy of the Koran and often carry it with me on my travels. I have read through it several times and have found that I learn something new about Islam each time I read it. I have come to the conclusion that the Koran—if digested chronologically, in its entirety, or in connection with the author—is impossible to use to promote peace without performing semantic gymnastics.

After only a short glance at the teachings in the Koran, it becomes clear that, arguable or not, ISIS has a very strong case in using the Koran in support of its ideology.

American-Islamic Relations

> When we had arrived [in Cork], I made a request to Lord Inchaquoin to give me a passport for England. I took boat to Youghal and then embarked on the vessel *John Filmer,* which set sail with 120 passengers. But before we had lost sight of land, we were captured by Algerine pirates, who put all the men in irons.[53]

Those were the memories of the Christian Reverend Devereux Spratt, who was taken captive by Algerian Muslims during his voyage across the Irish Sea. Like other Europeans and Americans, Reverend Spratt and fellow believers were specifically targeted by the Muslims of the Barbary Coast of North Africa (modern-day Algeria, Morocco, Tunisia, and Libya) simply because they were Christians.

In 2006, Democrat Keith Ellison became the first Muslim to be elected to the U.S. Congress. Keith, who was born in Detroit, Michigan, and who converted to Islam during his time in university, decided that he was going to make history by taking his congressional oath with his hand upon a Koran instead of on a Bible. Very few Americans were aware of the fact; of those who were, only a handful knew what it meant for our country. In January 2007, Keith Ellison took his oath, placing his hand upon a copy of the Koran that was published in 1764 and that had belonged to Thomas Jefferson.

Congressman Ellison said that he chose to use Jefferson's copy of the Koran "because it showed that a visionary like Jefferson believed that wisdom could be gleaned from many sources."[54]

The congressman was right. Jefferson needed to learn everything that he could about Islam, but not because of the reasons Congressman Ellison mentioned. Instead, it was because Jefferson was about to launch the very first foreign war in American history, which was a war on terror.

The war on ISIS is not America's first encounter with fighting Islamic terrorists. As a former U.S. Marine, I have the "Marines' Hymn" etched into my brain. It begins, "From the Halls of Montezuma // to the shores of Tripoli...." We sing it so that we never forget the battles from yesteryear. One of those battles took the U.S. Marines to foreign soil for the first time to fight the same Islamic ideology that had enslaved Reverend Devereux Spratt.

Thomas Jefferson, the third president of the United States, obtained a personal copy of the Koran because he knew it was important to understand Islam before engaging in war against the Islamic terrorists.

At that time in history, Americans had had enough of war. They had just fought the British for independence and were fatigued. However, the Muslims in northern Africa had other plans for them.

Not many Europeans and Americans know this, but as many as 1.5 million Americans and Europeans were enslaved by Muslims in North Africa during the late 1700s and early 1800s. North African Muslims regularly launched raids in Europe, taking men, women, and children from their homes and dragging them back to Africa by ship to sell on the open market. American merchant ships were also regularly attacked, and every passenger was put up for sale. As we read in *The Pirate Coast: Thomas Jefferson, the First Marines, and the Secret Mission of 1805*, "Sura 47 of the Koran allowed these Muslim attackers to enslave and ransom any of these captives. Young Italian women would fetch more than the men in the flesh markets of Tunis and Algiers."[55] We also learn the following:

> Men were usually peddled near naked, or in dangly shirts, in an outdoor auction; women could be inspected privately in stalls nearby. Unlike slave auctions in the southern United States, male buyers here openly acknowledged lustful desires for their human purchases; matrons inspected the women, and virgins were sold at a steep premium, often with a written guarantee.[56]

Before Jefferson became president, he and John Adams met with Abdul Rahman Adja, the Tripoli (Libya today) ambassador to Britain. Jefferson had inquired of the ambassador why his government was so hostile to the new government of America, when nothing had been done to provoke aggression. His response was reported to the Continental Congress:

> It was founded on the laws of their Prophet; that it was written in their Koran; that all nations who should not have acknowledged their authority were sinners; that it was their right and duty to make war upon them wherever they could be found, and to make slaves of all they could take as prisoners; and that every Mussulman who was slain in battle was sure to go to Paradise.[57]

When Jefferson was president, the United States was not involved in Middle Eastern oil; it was not sending support to Israel (Israel did not exist); it was not supporting Palestinian sanctions; nor had the nation ever been involved in the crusades; yet the United States was still the recipient of terrorist attacks. This historical fact tosses out the notion that, if world powers would stop meddling in terrorist activities, terrorists would just go away and leave people alone.

The situation was even worse than just the enslavement of Americans and the terrorist attacks. Though the United States had been able to gain independence from Britain, it became financially enslaved to the Muslim countries, paying 20 percent of its GDP to the Barbary pirate countries in order to keep their citizens from being taken as slaves. This was even worse than "taxation without representation." Furthermore, even though the United States paid the fee to the Muslims, the pirates continued to capture ships and Americans.

President Jefferson had had enough, and he sent in the Marines. The Marines knew that the Barbary pirates had a method of decapitating their enemy in the same way that Muhammad had done, so they wore strips of leather around their necks to protect themselves. This earned them the nickname "leathernecks," which is still used to this day. Through the First and Second Barbary Wars, the United States was released from paying tribute to the Barbary States.

3. When Was Islam Established?

Now we will consider Islamic growth throughout history. How did countries become Islamic? How has the religion spread? Do the trends President Jefferson saw two hundred years ago still exist today? If it is true that the Koran and the prophet Muhammad are at the root of Islamic violence, are there "symptoms" that prove that? Because, as with an illness, symptoms can help identify the cause of a problem. You can call the seed of a cherry tree the seed of an apple tree all you like; but when the seed grows and becomes a tree, it will have no choice but to produce cherries.

Since its inception, Islam has been an agent of change in neighboring cultures and societies. Consequently, understanding the historical spread of Islam will help us to better understand the Islamic State.

When Muhammad died in 632 AD, Islam had gained a number of military victories; through these victories, the new religion had gained the wealth it needed to sustain itself. The trajectory that had been started by the prophet continued ripping through the Arabian Peninsula. Within only a few years after Muhammad's death, his followers had invaded and conquered Christian, Jewish, Hindu, Buddhist, and Zoroastrian lands. These people groups were given the choice to convert, pay *jizya*, or die. Sound familiar? Not even one country converted to Islam without the threat of force.

Twenty-five years following the death of Muhammad, Muslim armies had conquered, taken over, and successfully converted twenty-eight modern-day countries to Islam.

War was in the DNA of the newly established Islamic religion. Though it may not have been the way the prophet had initially intended to spread Islam in the early days of Mecca, coercion and war proved to be the most profitable and successful methods of conversion. War produced results.

The prophet led by example during the early days. Through the raids and the bloody battles with Mecca, Muhammad communicated a message to his followers that conquering countries and selling slaves was a good method of financing future campaigns.

The leaders who took over following the prophet's death were known as "caliphs," or spiritual, political, and military leaders in the order of Muhammad. Not one of them displayed a message of love, peace, and reconciliation. They led military campaigns to conquer and spread the caliphate. This is the primary goal of al-Baghdadi, as well.

Islam spread like the plague. Iran's Zoroastrians were conquered. Syrians, Iraqis, and Egyptians, many of them Christians, were conquered. The Arabian Peninsula, parts of Asia and Asia Minor, and North Africa were conquered. Israel and Cyprus were conquered. The Christian capital of Constantinople was blasted with bloodshed.

Soon, Europe, sapped of energy and resources from its battles with the plague, was attacked from every direction except the north. Spain soon fell. Italy was attacked, and Sicily was taken over. Rome was attacked, forcing the Roman garrison and the pope to run.

Four of the five main centers of Christianity were attacked by Islamic jihadists and were eventually conquered. Muslims cut off European trade routes to Asia. Eastern sea routes were too dangerous, which led to desperate explorative trips in search of alternative routes. One of those desperate attempts led to the accidental founding of the Americas by Christopher Columbus, who at first thought he had found another route to India that would bypass the dangerous and risky Muslim countries. In this way, Islam actually contributed to the European discovery of America.

In an attempt to point out that Christians are also guilty of hideous war crimes, people will bring up the crusades; but, keep in mind that, at the time of the first crusade, Islam had been invading and destroying Christian countries for four centuries. After four hundred long, hard years of being attacked, conquered, raped, pillaged, and enslaved (longer than the United States has been a country), Europe finally launched its offense, which is credited with saving Europe from being forced into Islam.

When Muslims conquered a country, their defeat was absolute. The invading armies were imperialistic and colonialist. They expected to benefit from their efforts by living off their conquests. Men were slaughtered, women were raped, and children were taken as slaves. Raped women gave birth to children who grew up to be slaves, resulting in a constant supply of workers and income. Everyone was forced into Islamic society. In most cases, everyone was forced to either convert or pay *jizya*.

It was not long before France was under attack, which was a turning point in the march of Islam.

It should be noted that this history should not be used to demonize Islam. Bloodshed, rape, and enslavement were not unique to the Islamists. They were common practices during that time. Some Christian armies practiced rape, murder, and theft. The actions displayed by the Muslim armies, which would be considered barbaric today, were not out of the ordinary. In fact, it could be argued that, in some cases, Muslims were liberating people who were under the control of an equally tyrannical government; for this reason, many indigenous people welcomed the invading Muslims with open arms, hoping for relief and justice.

The point here is not to evaluate the actions of the Muslim armies in comparison to today's standards. The rules of war dictated by the Geneva Convention cannot be used to assess the practices of the Muslim armies during that time. No, the primary point is that the spread of Islam did not take place in a peaceful manner. The historic expansion of Islam was not any different from the example set by the prophet Muhammad and the teachings of the Koran.

This could not be any more distinct from the early spread of Christianity, when the blood of Christian martyrs was sacrificed instead of the blood of an enemy. Early Christianity was built on the foundations of nonviolence and self-sacrifice. After all, Jesus Christ, who never killed or smote another human being, willingly gave His life on the cross for the sins of all people. In contrast, the Islamic military warrior Muhammad held a sword soaked in the blood of his enemy.

4. Where Do the Majority of Muslims Live?

If we leave the history of Islam behind, forget about the actions and deeds of the founding prophet, and ignore the Koranic teachings of war and jihad, would we find Islam to be a religion of peace? Has there been a change in Islam over the last 1,400 years? If we evaluate present-day Muslim countries and examine the empirical evidence, will we find confirmation that Islam is a peaceful religion?

Just a cursory glance at contemporary Muslim countries would show an honest observer a couple of things and bring to mind some questions. First, have any significant educational, medical, technological, or scientific endeavors originated from Muslim countries? (This does not mean that there haven't been any.) When you think of computer giants, do any Islamic brand names come to mind?

Kuwait, like Saudi Arabia, is a very wealthy country with access to lots of water, beaches, and sunshine. But would you book a summer beach vacation in either one of those countries? On any given day, international travel warnings are riddled with notices to avoid countries that are governed by Islam.

Travel + Leisure magazine publishes an annual listing of the world's most dangerous countries. This list has nothing to do with religion; rather, its purpose is simply to warn travelers of dangers that exist in certain countries.

Any guess where the majority of travel dangers are? More than two-thirds of the most dangerous places are Muslim nations.[58]

Are the writers for *Travel + Leisure* magazine Islamophobic? Maybe there is another reason why Muslim nations are not creating warm and fuzzy feelings for visitors.

When observing Muslim countries, perhaps you think of the most moderate Muslim nations like Indonesia, Malaysia, Turkey, or United Arab Emirates (Dubai). However, in some Muslim nations like Malaysia, witnessing about Jesus with Muslims is strictly prohibited, "all conversions must be affirmed by a Sharia court, and the [conversion] process requires converts to spend three months in a re-education centre [to encourage] reconsideration."[59]

To most first-time visitors, Dubai appears to be a beacon of freedom; but if you were a freedom-seeking pilgrim, then Dubai would be a huge disappointment to you. Only expatriates are allowed freedom of religion, and only as long as they respect local customs. Furthermore, local citizens are executed for leaving the Islamic religion.[60]

Saudi Arabia, Pakistan, Iran, Afghanistan, Sudan, Mauritania, and Maldives are Muslim countries where atheists can be executed.[61] In modern Muslim countries, we see that Islam, like the mob, is the only major world religion that retains its members by threatening to kill anyone who decides to leave.

And the methods of execution are still practiced as they were in the days of Muhammad. In August 2014 alone, Saudi Arabia, a so-called friend of the West, executed twenty-two people, cutting off their heads with a sword. Some of these victims had been accused of practicing sorcery, which oftentimes means that they did not practice the same kind of Islam as the state.[62]

Saudi Arabia frequently finds itself on human rights abuse reports. Saudi Arabia is home to Mecca, the destination of every Muslim who makes the pilgrimage. Is it possible to explain away the reports by saying that they are extremists? As activist Anne-Marie Waters said in discussing whether Islam is a peaceful religion, "Calling Saudi Arabia the extreme fringe of Islam is like calling the Vatican the extreme fringe of Catholicism."[63]

Stoning, called "rajam" in Arabic, is either a legal form of punishment or practiced extrajudicially in sixteen Muslim countries, including Saudi Arabia, the UAE, Qatar, Indonesia, and Brunei.[64]

These examples are from "moderate" Muslim countries. Things look much worse when we begin to examine countries that are labeled as more extreme. The argument is often made that only 1 percent of Muslims worldwide are extremists. But Islam is the second largest religion in the world, and it currently has more than a billion and a half followers. That means that more than 15 million Muslims across the globe are extremists. That 1 percent argument does not make people feel any safer about Islamic extremists.

Even a quick look at the practices of Muslim countries does not bode well for the argument that Islam is a religion of peace. Not one Muslim country is a beacon of peace and freedom to the rest of the world.

5. Why Islam?

Incentives are used to prompt people toward certain behaviors. Incentives can be found in every religion. However, in Islam, it is clear that some people favor incentives of violence. Throughout the Koran, Muhammad promises those fighting for him that Allah will reward them with salvation and a paradise full of virgins. (See Koran 44:51–56; 52:17–20; 55:46–78.)

Interestingly, even Muhammad doubted his salvation; he said very clearly, "Nor do I know what will be done with me or with you" (Koran 46:9). According to Muhammad, the only way for a Muslim to secure a place in paradise is to become a martyr in jihad. This promise is found in Koran 9:111, which oddly resembles the date of the infamous terrorist attack on America—9/11/2001.

Charity is compulsory in Islam, but it does not guarantee salvation. Peace is preached by Islamic statesmen, yet it does not guarantee salvation. Only martyrdom can do that.

My hope is that, in any discussion regarding Islam, you will use these five *w*'s as a guide to understanding the religion, and you will discover the truth yourself.

FIVE

Christians in Iraq and Syria

David, a Back to Jerusalem representative in Baton Rouge, Louisiana, opened up his e-mail to find a prayer request from Iraq. "I want to read a prayer request," David said to the Back to Jerusalem team, trying to pull himself together. His hands were shaking, and his voice broke as he struggled to contain his emotions.

"This e-mail is from missionaries who are being attacked by ISIS and are asking to be showered in prayer. ISIS has taken over the town that they are in today. They said that ISIS is systematically going house to house to all the Christians and asking the children to denounce Jesus. So far, not one child has; but, consequently, all have been killed."

David, himself a father and a grandfather, could not keep his lip from quivering as he read on. "The UN has withdrawn, and the missionaries are on their own. They are determined to stick it out for the sake of the families—even if it means their own death. They are very afraid and have no idea how to even begin ministering to the families who have seen their children killed; but the missionaries say that, for some reason, God has called them to be His voice and hands at this place and time."

After listening to David speak and contemplating what was going on in Iraq, I shared a short message from the book of Esther:

> *For if thou altogether holdest thy peace at this time, then will relief and deliverance arise to the Jews from another place, but thou and thy father's house will perish: and who knoweth* ***whether thou art not come to the kingdom for such a time as this?*** (Esther 4:14 ASV)

This message now seemed to be more than a suburban biblical appetizer served on a cul-de-sac cracker. The words in the e-mail were not stories from several thousand years ago but were fresh from the field.

As Christians in the West, we can, as Esther was tempted to do, stay in the comfort of our castle and remain silent, or we can respond to the crisis of our time. If we remain silent, relief and deliverance will arise "*from another place.*"

The history of Christians in Iraq and Syria is not a new one. In fact, their story goes back thousands of years to the beginning of the apostolic movement following the resurrection of Jesus Christ.

Moreover, the modern-day killing and torture of the Christians in Iraq did not start with ISIS. After the capture of Saddam Hussein in 2003, a concoction of persecution was released on Iraqi Christians. If it wasn't al-Qaeda in Iraq targeting believers in Mosul, then it was the Shia warlords. If it was not the Shia Muslims, then it was the Sunni insurgents. There are not many Iraqi groups that have *not* joined in the persecution against Christians, who are like the family dog that everyone feels entitled to kick.

In August 2004, right after the overthrow of Saddam Hussein, persecutors bombed five churches in Baghdad and Mosul, and eleven people were killed. Before the end of the year, two other churches were bombed. And the violence continues: Since the end of 2004, insurgents have bombed sixty churches.[65]

Pastors and bishops also became major targets. In June 2007, in Mosul, a priest and three deacons were shot dead for refusing to convert to Islam. Archbishop Paulos Faraj Rahho was abducted, thrown into the trunk of a car, and killed; afterward, his body was thrown into a shallow grave. Since the capture of Saddam Hussein, extremist groups have kidnapped young children from Christian families and have kept them for ransom.

In Mosul, Muslims pointed out Christian households to ISIS, so that their homes could be marked with the Arabic *n*, much as the Star of David was used to mark Jewish homes in Hitler's Germany.

Yet the persecution of Christians in northern Iraq did not start with the fall of Saddam Hussein. These Christians have been persecuted for their faith for generations, dating back to the days when the Muslims first invaded Iraq.

Iraqi Christians have survived every single major invasion by the most powerful armies in the world—until now. It is important to note that most Iraqi Christians are not Arabs, as most assume; neither are they Kurds. They are a mix of Assyrian and Babylonian, and their roots can actually be traced back to the city of Ashur, the ancient capital of Assyria, located on the west bank of the Tigris River. They have Semitic roots. (See Genesis 10:22.)

The early inhabitants of Iraqi, known in ancient times as Mesopotamia, contributed many great inventions to civilization.[66] In contrast, Islam is, arguably, one of the greatest enemies of innovation and creativity. Arguments are made in academia on a regular basis about the great contributions of Muslim thinkers and innovators throughout history. Their arguments are misleading, at best, and flat-out lies, at worst. Many of the kingdoms that Islam conquered were more advanced before they were taken over by Islam than they are today. This may be a hard analysis of Islam, but how else can a person explain why there are no significant medical, scientific, or technological discoveries being made by those in Islamic countries today? Islam established itself through superiority on the battlefield.

Development and innovation existed in many of the great empires prior to Islamic invasion. After invasion, some residual inventions and innovations took place; but, over time, they were smothered by Islam. It can be argued that many inventions that have been attributed to Muslims were acquired through looting and robbing, both of which have been synonymous with Islam since the religion's founding by Muhammad. Muslims have benefited from exposure to other cultures—for example, it has contributed to a rise in their standard of living—however, the reverse is not true.

Iraqi Christians therefore have a very rich cultural history, but they have been smothered by Islamic rule for so many generations that their only concern has been survival.

Islam is not, and has never been, in their culture. Iraqi and Syrian Christians speak the ancient language that Jesus spoke; and, again, it is thought that their roots date back to the days of the world's earliest Christians.

Isaiah wrote,

> *In that day shall there be a highway out of Egypt to Assyria, and the Assyrian shall come into Egypt, and the Egyptian into Assyria, and the Egyptians shall serve with the Assyrians. In that day shall Israel be the third with Egypt and with Assyria, even a blessing in the midst of the land: whom the* L*ORD* *of hosts shall bless, saying, Blessed be Egypt my people, and*

Assyria the work of my hands, and Israel mine inheritance.
(Isaiah 19:23–25 KJV)

ISIS has been paying particular attention to Christian communities, which shows that its aim is not merely to gain control of the land in Iraq and Syria but also to cleanse it of all Christians and Jews. It has already inflicted the most gruesome war on Christians—worse than any persecution in recent times. The Christians who have fled from ISIS compose the largest mass flight of Christians in the Middle East since the massacres in Turkey after WWI.[67]

Shortly after taking over the city of Mosul, al-Baghdadi announced that Christians had until Saturday, July 19, to convert, pay *jizya,* or leave the city. According to the letters that were handed out, if Christians did not choose one of those options, "the only [other] option [was] the sword."[68]

Even if a Christian converted to Islam, he was not spared the horrors of ISIS. A copy of one of ISIS's letters sent out in Mosul stated that giving up the unmarried daughters of a family was the duty of jihad.

The letter stated,

> After liberation of the State of Nineveh, and the welcome shown by the people of the state to their brotherly mujahideen, and after the great conquest, and the defeat of the Safavid [Persian] troops in the State of Nineveh, and its liberation, and Allah willing, it will become the headquarters of the mujahideen. Therefore we request that the people of this state offer their unmarried women so they can fulfill their duty of jihad by sex to their brotherly mujahideen. Failure to comply with this mandate will result in enforcing the laws of Sharia on them.[69]

Mosul used to have the largest Christian population in Iraq, which had lasted for about 2,000 years. Now, basically all of the Christians are gone. Ancient Christian manuscripts were destroyed, and relics and artifacts were stolen from the churches and religious sites. And all forty-five Christian institutions in Mosul were destroyed or occupied by ISIS. Yet, out of all the places that were destroyed, there was one that stood out from all the rest.

When I first heard about Mar Behnam Monastery being destroyed, in my mind it was lost with all the other monasteries that had been destroyed or occupied. It was just another monastery, until I heard the other name that it was known by—Monastery of the Martyrs.

Islamic jihadists did not know that, when they arrived in the Christian town of Qaraqosh on June 10, 2014, they were not the first Muslim marauders to occupy the city. They were not the first people to kill Christians in that area.

The monastery was named after Mar Behnam, whose father had been a powerful king three hundred years before Muhammad was born. One day, while hunting in the forest, Mar Behnam came across a crazy "Jesus freak." It is unknown whether his hunting trip had been successful, but Mar Behnam listened to the words and teaching of the crazy Christian and then asked for some proof. The Christian told Mar Behnam to return with his sister Sarah, who had leprosy.

Mar Behnam ran home and got his sister so that the one who had talked about Christ could pray for her. The Christian baptized her, and she was immediately healed of leprosy. Afterward, both Mar and Sarah were filled with joy and gave their hearts to Jesus.

However, their rejoicing in her healing was short-lived, ceasing when their father found out that his two children had converted to Christianity. He demanded that both of them deny the name of Jesus. They refused to deny Christ, so, much like the Iraqi Christians are doing today, they fled for their lives.

They did not make it far. Their flight was intercepted by a group of men who worked for their father the king. They killed Mar Behnam and Sarah, along with forty other new believers.

The king's anger died with his son and his daughter. His children had been royalty, yet they had refused to deny the name of Jesus in exchange for comfort. He was unable to sleep and was tormented. Then he became possessed. He had killed his own son and daughter, and he went insane!

The king's wife sought out the same Jesus freak who had led her son to Jesus and healed her daughter of leprosy. After the king had talked to him for only a brief time, he was healed of his insanity and gave his heart to Jesus. After being baptized, he wanted to do something to remember what had happened to his two children, who had bravely given their hearts to Christ. So, in their memory, he built Mar Behnam Monastery.

When ISIS stormed into that monastery on that Sunday morning, the monks were preparing for their services. They were brutally attacked and forced to leave. The monks begged to take some of the important artifacts and literature with them, but their request was denied, and they left with only the clothes on their back.

The story of the monastery teaches a message that ISIS might not be aware of: The love of Jesus Christ never forces anyone into conversion. Jesus triumphed over evil not by fighting his enemies but by sacrificing Himself for all mankind.

Just because ISIS has destroyed every church building in its path does not mean that it has successfully destroyed *the* church. The body of Christ does not exist in a building; it is composed of the followers of Christ both of today and of years past. Death cannot destroy the body of Christ.

ISIS may have kicked out all of the Christians in the areas under its control, but it cannot destroy the good news. ISIS members victoriously rejoice in the streets when they kill Christians; but, even in death, there is victory for those who believe in Jesus. When Jesus gave His life, hanging on the cross and taking His last breath, the enemy must have rejoiced victoriously. Little did he know that Jesus had purchased the salvation of mankind when He shed His blood on that cross. And He conquered the grave when He was resurrected.

ISIS and Biblical Prophesy

ISIS launched its Northern Iraq Offensive on June 5, 2014. Al-Baghdadi had his eyes set on Mosul, Iraq's second largest city, which was considered the Christian capital of the country. He regarded Mosul as a black spot in the heart of Islam, and he gave the order to launch the most significant offensive to date in the battle in Iraq.

Iraq's prime minister, Nouri al-Maliki, scoffed at the idea that the city of two million could be taken by what he considered to be a ragtag group compared to the Iraqi Special Operations Forces.

In the early morning hours of June 6, hundreds of ISIS jihadists jumped into pickup trucks and raced eastward toward Mosul under the cover of darkness. The black flags of ISIS were mounted but could not be seen in the darkness. Only the clinging of racing truck engines and the clanging of bouncing metal truck beds could be heard as they made their advance.

The Iraqi Army knew that ISIS was coming. Outnumbering the ISIS jihadists and having both the equipment and the backing of the Iraqi government did not give them any comfort. In fact, the troops started to slip out of the city at night, abandoning their posts.

As ISIS approached, the guards that were posted on roads outside the city, two guards per post, were not able to stop the vehicles. Within an hour, the fighters were swarming throughout the city and engaging in urban warfare. The ISIS fighters had momentum and esprit de corps on their side.

There should have been several thousand troops protecting the citizens of Mosul from the invasion; but the Iraqi army was running thin due to mass desertion and poor positioning. Mosul was naked before her enemies.

On the eve of the attack, knowing that a slaughter was about to take place, Kurdish fighting forces had offered more than once to provide aid, but the Iraqi president had declined their offer.

ISIS fighters littered the road with dead bodies. Many of the bodies were discovered to have been blindfolded with their hands tied, indicating that they had been executed. The bodies of decapitated police officers served as a warning to others. ISIS's message did not fall on deaf ears. The Iraqi Army systematically retreated until it had completely abandoned the city.

"Our leaders betrayed us," one angry Iraqi soldier said. "The commanders left the military behind. When we woke up, all the leaders had left."[70]

Once ISIS had control over Mosul, the banks and businesses were looted. ISIS was able to get immediate access to almost half a billion dollars in cash and valuables at the bank.[71]

Mosul seemed to be just another city in Iraq. However, when ISIS took it over, it was no longer referred to by its modern name, Mosul; instead, it was called by its ancient name: Nineveh.

Nineveh, an ancient Mesopotamian city, used to be the largest city in the world. The Bible tells how Noah's great-grandson Nimrod founded the city long before the days of ISIS:

> *And* [Noah's grandson] *Cush begat Nimrod: he began to be a mighty one in the earth. He was a mighty hunter before Jehovah: wherefore it is said, Like Nimrod a mighty hunter before Jehovah. And the beginning of his kingdom was Babel, and Erech, and Accad, and Calneh, in the land of Shinar. Out of that land he went forth into Assyria, and builded Nineveh.* (Genesis 10:8–11 ASV)

Many biblical scholars consider Nimrod to be the world's first tyrannical ruler. Nimrod, the founder of the city of Mosul, was the grandson of Ham, who dishonored his father, Noah. *"And Ham, the father of Canaan, saw the nakedness of his father, and told his two brethren without"* (Genesis 9:22). According to the Bible, when Noah awoke after his drunkenness, he was furious at what his son had done. He said, *"Cursed be Canaan; a servant of servants shall he be unto his brethren"* (Genesis 9:25 ASV). Canaan's son Nimrod was, therefore, a recipient of Noah's curse upon Ham.

According to Judaic teaching, Abraham's father, Terah, was a loyal servant to Nimrod. Because of the fear of one day being overthrown by a descendant of Shem, Nimrod tried to have Abraham killed.[72]

Nimrod was a powerful, skillful hunter, and he successfully built the first kingdom and a great city. He is one of the earliest examples of a leader who had a thirst to eliminate the lineage of the coming Savior, similar to that of King Herod's and the Egyptian pharaoh's.

The curse of Ham was upon Nimrod, but not in the way that kept him from obtaining power, wealth, and fame. Just the opposite. Nimrod was the most powerful, influential, wealthy, and famous person of his time.

Under Nimrod's control, there was no democracy. He had absolute power, and it seems that he even challenged the seat of God in attempting to build the Tower of Babel.

From Nimrod's ancient soil of Iraq emerged the five most powerful empires the world had ever seen—one of which was the great city of Babylon, where the Jews were taken into slavery after the city of Jerusalem had been conquered.

The five empires that emerged from Nimrod's Iraq were:

1. The Sumer Empire
2. The Babylonian Empire
3. The Assyrian Empire
4. The Neo-Babylonian Empire
5. The Abbasid Caliphate

The fifth empire to come from Iraqi soil was the Abbasid Caliphate; and, like ISIS, it came to power by attacking the morals of the ruling Muslims of the land. The first thing that the Abbasid Caliphate did was move to the capital city from Syria to Iraq. The Abbasid Caliphate ruled during what is considered to be the golden age of Islam, a period of time that ISIS would like to go back to.

The history of Iraq is not a bunch of jargon to ISIS. The Islamic State grasps it and holds it dear. It is driven by the history of Muhammad and Islam—from the beheadings to the conquered territory.

Its Achilles' heel is that its actions and motives can easily be predicted by students of Islamic history. ISIS favors history over strategy. ISIS has been strategic, no doubt, but it would never sacrifice historical value and significance for strategy. If ISIS had to choose between the two, history would win every time.

The Assyrian Empire was based in Mosul, and ISIS is all too familiar with the story of Jonah and Nineveh, which is also told in Koranic teachings. According to the Koran, the ancient city of Nineveh was knee-deep in idol worship, and the prophet Jonah

(Yunus) tried to share about Allah; but the people rejected him, so he went into a rage and left the city. After leaving, he was swallowed up by a large fish and spit back out. (See Koran 37:140–145.) Jonah returned to the city of Nineveh, and, this time, the people accepted Allah. Because they accepted him willingly, they were allowed to live. (See Koran 37:148.)

The end of surah 37 is not about Jonah, though. It reveals how Christians (or those who believe that God is begotten) will be dealt with. You see, disaster was averted for the Ninevites who accepted Allah during the days of Jonah, but it would come again for the Ninevites who rejected Allah in favor of the teachings of the begotten Savior.

ISIS believes that the attack on Mosul, the former city of Nineveh, was a punishment from Allah, not from ISIS. Militant Muslims believe that they are a tool in Allah's hand. The Christians, Jews, and other idol worshipers in Mosul were bound to be punished, and Allah called caliph al-Baghdadi to carry out his punishment.

ISIS is worse than the Third Reich. The main difference between the two is capability. The Third Reich destroyed more because it had the provision to do so. At first, ISIS lacked the provision to carry out large-scale attacks, but that situation changed overnight when it took the city of Mosul. It obtained a geographical location that is important for controlling northern Iraq. It also gained immediate access to the resources of the banks and businesses. It gained many strategic benefits by taking Mosul.

When ISIS captured Mosul and began calling it Nineveh, many observers realized that the battle for Mosul had more than just strategic value; it became obvious that there was historical value, as well.

If any of this sounds a bit far-fetched to you, and if you still consider ISIS to be just a bunch of ignorant terrorists who would not know a Wikipedia page from a Hawaiian Island screen saver, then consider the following.

In the third week of July, a month after ISIS gained control of Mosul, one of the local residents stood outside and filmed the destruction of one of the most historically significant relics in northern Iraq—the tomb of Jonah. The man who filmed the video said, "No, no, no. Prophet Jonah is gone. God, these scoundrels."[73]

In the Bible, Jonah was sent to Nineveh to warn the people about the impending doom of God if they did not repent. Tradition holds that he was buried in the city at the hill of the prophet Jonah. A mosque was built over the tomb, and it was eventually turned into a shrine that was frequented by Muslims from all over the world.[74]

According to Sam Hardy, a professor at the American University in Rome, ISIS is determined to destroy "basically pretty much anything in the Bible."[75] To ISIS, any monument or destination that is paid homage represents a type of idolatry. Not only does the tomb of Jonah represent idolatry, but it also has dangerous symbolism. Jonah had been inside a fish for three days before he was spat out, sharing parallel testimony to Jesus' resurrection on the third day. Therefore, the Mosque of the Prophet Yunus had to be destroyed.

Recently released was video footage of a black-clad ISIS jihadist inside the shrine with a sledgehammer. In the video, he wildly swings the sledgehammer over and over, chipping away at four green concrete graves and damaging the revered site.

On the day the mosque was destroyed, locals were kept away from the shrine. The road was closed 500 meters from the site.[76] The structure was strapped with explosives, and in just a moment, the location that had served as a historical reference for Jews, Christians, and Muslims was blown to smithereens.

Al-Baghdadi must be very satisfied with his achievements in Mosul. The city is under his complete control, and Sharia law is now the supreme law of the citizenry. ISIS patrols the streets, ensuring that everyone is abiding by its strict teachings and interpretation of the Koran.

Though the future of Mosul is still unknown, for the time being, it does not look as if ISIS will be removed anytime soon. The curse of Nimrod seems to have returned to the ancient city of Nineveh, reminding us of the prophesy in Nahum 3:7 (KJV): "*And it shall come to pass, that all they that look upon thee shall flee from thee, and say, Nineveh is laid waste: who will bemoan her? Whence shall I seek comforters for thee?*"

SIX

Kurdistan

We arrived at the newly built, world-class Erbil International Airport in Iraq just after four in the morning on a Turkish Air flight from Istanbul. No visas were needed. The entire immigration process was one of the fastest and most hassle-free experiences I have ever encountered. It rivaled even Singapore's, which is known around the world for its order and expediency. We were greeted outside by new taxis lined up to take us weary, early morning travelers where we needed to go.

"Where you go?" a short, stout man asked me in broken English with a heavy Kurdish accent. He was holding a radio handset, obviously hoping we would not waste his time with a delayed answer.

"Dohuk," I responded as quickly as I could.

"Dohuk? OK, no problem," he said in a matter-of-fact tone.

He was the new face of northern Iraq. I imagined he was not worried about ISIS, even though ISIS was only a short drive away. Instead, he worried only about getting us where we needed to go.

Before long, a 2014 Toyota SUV pulled up to take us to Dohuk in northern Iraq. The three-hour journey north skirted along the

ISIS battle lines into the northern mountains of Iraq, but at no time were we in danger. The roads between Erbil and Dohuk in northern Iraq were not pitted with potholes from bombs or wandering mortar shells. Instead, they were wide and spacious, reminiscent of county line highways in west Texas. They were freshly paved and provided a smooth ride. Modern white street light poles arched over every section of the highway to provide plenty of illumination for the travelers making the lonesome journey at four in the morning.

Large road signs with cardinal directions in both Arabic and English marked the way for even the most geographically challenged drivers. Homes and businesses dotted the mountainside on each side of the highway, by-products of the recent economic boom. Bright lights beamed from restaurants, shopping malls, and grocery stores.

This was not the Iraq that I had seen on TV. Northern Iraq had been all over the news, and my friends and family members had been deeply concerned about my safety when I told them that I was traveling there to meet and work with Iraqi refugees.

Erbil: The Booming Capital of Kurdistan

Erbil, the capital of Kurdistan in northern Iraq, is the city that the Americans wanted to see. For the life, blood, sweat, tears, and, at times, sacrifice that American soldiers dedicated in Iraq, Erbil was the treasured prize that they had been desperately waiting for. Erbil was the gem to be admired and to be proud of. It represented what the rest of Iraq failed to represent: freedom.

There are roughly 30 million Kurds who live throughout Iraq, Syria, Turkey, and Iran. They are considered to be the largest ethnic group in the world without their own country.[77] The Iraqi autonomous region of Kurdistan, like the rest of Iraq, is rich in oil; so, it offers cheap fuel for incoming and outgoing flights. Even at the height of the ISIS invasion, Erbil International Airport remained open. Turkish Airlines daily flies jumbo jets filled to capacity to Erbil. Not only are there direct flights to Erbil from places like Turkey, Jordan, and Dubai, but there are also daily direct flights from Sweden and Germany. Erbil International Airport continues to maintain normal operations in spite of the operations of ISIS not far from the city.

Erbil is a bright, shining city on a hill. The Kurds have worked hard to create an investor-friendly environment, and, in 2006, they implemented a law that removed all restrictions for international investment, allowing foreign investors to be treated the same as local investors. In fact, there are several thousand foreign companies operating in Kurdistan, making it one of the top destinations for foreign investment in Iraq. "Erbil, the capital of Iraqi Kurdistan, has earned the title of the 'Dubai of Iraq' and has been named the tourist capital of the Arab world in 2014."[78]

Erbil's booming economy has its own stock exchange. The city is selling oil to places like Turkey without the control or permission of Baghdad. One businessman, making money hand over fist in Kurdistan, is building an exact replica of the American White House for his own private residence, unfazed by ISIS's threat the next city over.

Northern Iraq, which is now partly controlled by the Kurds and partly by ISIS, was the one of the first kingdoms and first metropolitan areas to be established by Nimrod in the Bible. Abraham passed through there on his journey from Ur of the Chaldees to Canaan. Thomas and Thaddeus planted churches in this region only a few years after the death of Christ. These churches still exist in some shape or form today. The land that the Kurds occupy is about as large as the state of Texas, and about as different from southern Iraq as Italy is from Holland.

However, as stated above, the Kurds, unlike the Iraqis, do not have their own country. The Kurds have their own government, their own prime minister, their own president, their own economy, and their own military. All of this might seem odd; it is even harder to explain. The Kurds have a nation but not a land. They have a government but not a country. They have an army but not an officially recognized military. It is a bit like Taiwan is to China. Iraqi efforts against ISIS have failed, but Kurdish efforts have been extremely effective against the terrorist organization.

At every hotel and public building in Kurdistan, the Kurdish flag is flying high and proud. Visitors may feel as if they have left Iraq, but they have not (yet, somehow, they have).

The Kurds have been a persecuted people group for generations. They have been suppressed and persecuted by the Syrians, the Turks, the Iranians, and Iraqis. They have come very close to obtaining independence on many occasions in the recent past, but they have always fallen short for one reason or another. The Kurdish people have been labeled as terrorists by most of their Arab neighbors, and they have been demonized by some of the Islamic countries where they now reside; but, in their hearts, they are simple farmers and mountain dwellers who want only to be left alone to live their lives and to raise their families.

The Kurds, like so many others, were taken completely off guard by the ISIS invasion. When ISIS began to move across northern Iraq, it was hitting fast and hard. The Kurds, falling under the command of the Iraqi government, were not prepared.

A small ISIS force attacked the Kurdish territory and made huge advances in very little time. Before long, ISIS had overrun Kurdish forces and conquered the western towns of Sinjar and Makhmour. It had even come as close as Gwer, which is only fifteen miles from the economically booming city of Erbil. The quick victory by ISIS struck panic and fear in the hearts of the Kurds.

Unlike Westerners, who sat at home and watched this all unfold on the evening news, the fearful Kurds sat in their homes with their children, wondering if they would be the next victims.

"It was about two o'clock in the morning," one former resident of Sinjar told me through a translator in November 2014. "I was sleeping, when, suddenly, I heard explosions and machine-gun fire. ISIS was attacking our village. I feared for my family. I had a rifle in the house, so I jumped up, grabbed my rifle, and ran outside to fight."

He paused to take another drag on his cigarette. He didn't look at me or at the Kurdish translator for a moment as he reflected on that night, which seemed still fresh in his mind. I could tell from his facial expressions that the memory was raw. The former resident of Sinjar was in his late forties or early fifties and was balding. He sat outside on a half-built concrete wall across the road from the half-built structure that he and his family had used as shelter.

"I fought them until I ran out of bullets. I didn't have anything else to fight with. ISIS was well-equipped. They even had tanks! How was I supposed to fight that?"

"They had tanks?" I asked in disbelief. I thought that maybe my translator had gotten it wrong.

"Yes," he responded, using his arms to imitate the tanks or heavily armored vehicles rolling into his village. "We couldn't fight any longer, so I ran back to my home and grabbed my family, and we ran into the mountains. We all were able to get away except for my brother's daughter. She was taken. We have not heard anything from her. Most likely, she was sold to someone or given away to be a bride of ISIS."

"My daughter hurt her legs during the escape," he said, pointing to a young girl sitting on the rocks. "She is not able to walk. We don't have any medicine to give her, and we don't have the money to take her to a doctor."

ISIS seized Mosul and the Mosul dam, giving it control of the region's water supply. It was humiliating for the Iraqi government and even more so for the Kurdish people, who pride themselves in being fierce warriors.

Like everyone else, the Kurdish fighters were taken by surprise by the shock attack of ISIS. Diplomats, politicians, and strategists had been absolutely certain that ISIS would be unable to initiate such an attack. Very few were prepared for the invasion.

The Kurdish military fighters are called the "peshmerga," which means "those who face death." The Iraqi government immediately blamed all its problems with the ISIS advances on the Kurds, paying no mind to the fact that Iraqi soldiers had folded like cards when the ISIS fighters had arrived.

This has caused a big split between the Iraqi government in Baghdad and the Kurdish government in Erbil. The Iraqi prime minister, Nouri al-Maliki, accused the Kurds of providing safety to ISIS and other Sunni insurgents.[79]

The peshmerga fighters, ignoring the hostility in Baghdad, immediately swung into action and went on the offensive, pushing back ISIS and taking back several towns it had occupied. Instead of being excited that ISIS was being defeated, Prime Minister al-Maliki appeared on television and said, "Everything that has been changed on the ground must be returned."[80]

This was a direct blow against the Kurdish military, reminding them that they were not autonomous conquerors but were under the Iraqi government. "We can't stay silent over Irbil being a headquarters for Daesh [term used for ISIS], Baath, al-Qaida and the terrorists."[81]

Of course there was no evidence that the Kurds were helping ISIS. They had been the only ones fighting, and had actually taken ground back from ISIS. It was a strong statement that reflected the deep distrust the Iraqis have of the Kurds. It is almost as if Iraq would have rather had the land taken by ISIS than put into the hands of the Kurds.

The Iraqi prime minister knew what all other Islamic governments know: This could be an opportunity for the Kurdish people to solidify their independence. If ISIS conquered Iraqi territories, as well as Syrian territories, and the Kurds rushed in to the save the day, taking the territory back as no one else could, then the Kurds might just obtain their independence.

The major problem, of course, is that the Iraqi government has not been able to defeat ISIS. The Syrian government has not been able to defeat ISIS. ISIS continues to take more and more territory from these two countries. Only one group has been able to fight ISIS on equal ground and successfully defeat them—the Kurds, which leads people to ask why they do not yet have their own country.

Religion in Kurdistan

The Kurds are mainly Muslim, after having had the religion forced on them during generations of Islamic occupation, but they have also played a major part in Christian history. Kurdish Christians helped to write the Nicene Creed, the canonical doctrine that sets forth much of what Christians believe today. They were also very active Nestorians who sent missionaries out to regions all over the known world to share the good news of Jesus Christ. The Christian Kurds played very prominent roles in the spread of Christianity up until the seventh century, when jihad armies came marching into the territory, as ISIS is doing today.

Freedom and acceptance of different religions abound in Kurdistan in Iraq. Under a new law implemented by the leaders of the Kurdistan government, which exercises a great deal of autonomy, all religions will be taught and treated equally. Extensive knowledge of Islam is no longer required to graduate from high school. This means that Iraqi Christians living in Kurdistan have equal opportunities in business and government. Compared to other Sunni nations in the region, this is extremely uncommon, and, no doubt, has contributed to the economic boom. It has also contributed to the high absorption of refugees running from ISIS.

To anyone used to traveling in Muslim regions of the Middle East, Kurdistan does not have a lot of the signs of Islam. Islam definitely exists as the main religion, but it does not seem to be a significant part of everyday life.

"The people here are Kurdish first and Muslim second," explains Isak Nilsson, a Swedish humanitarian aid worker with Operation Mercy living in Dohuk. "It really impacts the way they treat others who live here, which is different than [what you see] when you go to another Arab region."[82]

The Kurdish people are not like the Arabs in the rest of the Middle East. First, they love Americans, and they are friends of Israel. Israel has pushed hard for the Kurdish people to receive their own land. America has partnered with them on several occasions to help them accomplish their own tasks in the Middle East, at little or no benefit to themselves. Unfortunately, the United States has also abandoned the Kurdish people over and over again.

I find it impossible to write objectively about the Kurds. They are an amazing people group that has endured so much, and they continue to be an inspiring model of perseverance. They have been used and abused in many ways, yet they continue to be the West's most reliable partner in the Middle East, outside of Israel.

Like a trusty neighbor, they have provided a protective covering for the persecuted people groups that have been attacked by ISIS. It seems odd that they are giving protection to persecuted minorities, since they, too, are often oppressed, yet they have provided aid to those in need.

After the ISIS assault, some Kurdish towns doubled in size due to the number of refugees. None of the refugees has been rejected. The Iraqi government has not been able to provide support or protection for its own people. They can barely protect their own capital city of Baghdad, which is in danger of falling at any time. It is only international support that keeps ISIS at bay there. That is not the case in Kurdistan.

Persecution of Kurdish Christians

At Back to Jerusalem in China, we receive prayer requests for persecuted Christians in Iraq on a consistent basis. One such request came in an e-mail that read,

> Dear brother,
>
> The Yazidi-Kurds from northern Iraq who have fled from ISIS have reached 13,000 in our camp. The numbers are increasing day by day. The biggest need is in the cities of Zakho and Duhok, where 450,000 Yazidi people are homeless and desperate for intervention.

A Kurdish pastor in Turkey whom I have been working with found himself swamped with requests for help in the Iraqi situation. I have collaborated with him to smuggle Bibles into Iran, and I knew that I could trust his evaluation of the situation. In the years I have known him, he has never sent me requests for assistance. But the following e-mail he sent me was different. He was desperate.

> The situation is critical, and, so far, the government has kept silent. Only volunteer groups like us are doing something to help. The governor and the district authorities

have not moved a feather to relieve the people's sorrow. Only the city hall led by the opposition party has been working hard to mobilize the population to host many Yazidi refugees in their homes.

These people are needy in every single way. Many of them have lost their relatives and need health care. Psychological counseling is needed. Even children and young people are in profound depression from dealing with the loss. It is clear that the hundreds of thousands of Yazidi Kurds who have lost their trust in their Muslim neighbors are unnoticed by the politicians of this country. We will not leave them alone. If the local authorities are the only ones helping them, then we want to support them to do a better job. This is a huge open door to show and share God's unconditional love and mercy, putting it into practice.

The pastor's heart touched my own. His e-mail communicated the destruction and pain that the black heart of man creates. There was a touch of hopelessness and despair in the beginning of the e-mail, but, before I had finished reading, the pastor's loyalty and commitment to the likeness of Jesus Christ radiated warmth and gave me hope that something could be done to fight back and help the Iraqis.

Though I had worked with the pastor, I had met him in person only one time. He is the pastor of a church in eastern Turkey, close to the border of Iran. He, too, is a refugee.

Eastern Turkey has a huge population of Kurds. In the 2010 earthquake that hit eastern Turkey, I worked closely with the mayor of the Turkish city of Van, Bekir Kaya, who was later accused of being a Kurdish rebel leader and put in prison.

ISIS has made huge advances in both Syria and Iraq. The immediate military solution of stopping the persecution of ISIS on minority groups in Iraq seems to rest with the Kurds, while the long-term solution to the ISIS problem is to bring in the gospel of Jesus Christ to change the hearts of men and women. The world community seems to have rejected both of these answers; as a result, ISIS continues to take over areas.

An American radio talk show personality, Glenn Beck, invited Erik Prince to speak on his show in October 2014. Erik Prince is one of the founders of the company Blackwater, as well as its former CEO. The company, now known as Academi, provides military services in high-risk areas. Erik is an expert in analyzing foreign military risks. On the program, he pointed out the link between Syria and Libya and gave the solution to fighting ISIS.

"Let me switch gears and go to ISIS," Glenn Beck said during his interview with Erik Prince. "We knew who these people were. We've known who they were for a very long time. The people in Benghazi that were killed, private contractors, we just left them behind, just discarded them. I think that we were running guns over to Syria—"

"Uh, no, actually—missiles," said Erik Prince, pointing out that missile trafficking was the main focus of the American operatives who were killed in Benghazi.

"Okay, there you go," Glenn said. He was clearly shocked at Erik's response. He thought they had been running guns. "Do you have anything on Benghazi that you want to share?"

"No, look, the reason that annex was there was that they were buying back missiles from the Libyans and shipping them to Syria."

"What should we be doing, Erik?" Glenn asked.

"Well, if the Assad regime were to fall right now, then ISIS would be running Syria, as well."

"Correct."

"You know, we could do the whole post analysis of what was done wrong that led to ISIS being in charge; but now, the people that we should be supporting vigorously are the Kurds. They have yet to receive any serious weapon systems, despite all the promises and assurances from the U.S. government. So these poor guys are still going head-to-head with ISIS, who captured five heavy divisions of American equipment—new state-of-the-art stuff and another three major logistics bases worth of ammunition, including...stingers, they have Hellfire missiles...that they captured from a resupply convoy coming to Baghdad from Kuwait. So, they are very well equipped to fight for years to come.

"The Kurds, on the other hand, are fighting with old Saddam-era stuff that they captured in the 90s. And they are completely outgunned and outmatched. They fight bravely, but it's hard to take on a fully armed vehicle with just an AK. That is not a fight you ever want to be in."[83]

The Kurds have used their military strength to free and to empower Christians. The fighting between the Kurds and ISIS stretches along a border area in northern Iraq that is almost seven hundred miles long.

At the moment, besides the international force in Baghdad, the only thing standing between ISIS taking over Iraq is the Kurds. ISIS knows this, and they hate the Kurds even more because of it.

"They shot my leg right here," one Yazidi man said, pointing to his left thigh. He leaned heavily on a cane to help maintain his balance. He was much too young to be walking with a cane. ISIS terrorists had shot him in the leg as he stood guard at a military post outside the town of Ba'ach with another Kurdish fighter.

"We were not fighting with the Kurds; we were placed out there by the Arabs. They put us out there, just the two of us. ISIS drove up in a car and shot me. They attack me because I was Kurdish."

His Kurdish partner took him to the hospital, which was not able to offer him much aid. They did not have the equipment to take the bullet out. "Half of it is still in there," he said, pointing to his leg.

He was Kurdish, so the Iraqi military put him in the very front of the fighting, at a post where he and his fellow Kurd were exposed to an attack. He was little more than cannon fodder for the Iraqi military.

I have driven through north Iraqi Kurdistan and have seen much of the southern border stretch of the Kurdish 600–700 mile front with ISIS. The Iraqi-Kurdistan territory, which is currently where the Kurds are holding back ISIS, is actually the demarcation of the proposed border of the Kurdish independent state.

As stated previously, the ISIS situation, as horrible as its reign of terror has been, has given the Kurds a very rare opportunity, and the rest of the Middle East knows it. Everyone in the region opposes what ISIS might be inadvertently giving to the Kurds—independent statehood.

The emergence of ISIS and the inability of Iraq and Syria to defeat them are changing the region in unpredictable ways. For decades, the governments of Syria, Iraq, Iran, and Turkey have inflicted trials and mass trauma on the Kurds. Indeed, there has been a history of massacres against the Kurdish people.

Iraqis have good reason to be concerned. Their treatment of the Kurds does not bode well for those hoping for loyalty from them in this crisis. In 1986, Saddam Hussein launched a murderous campaign throughout northern Kurdistan known as al-Anfal, which is named after a chapter in the Koran referring to Muhammad's victory over unbelievers. Between 1986 and 1989, several thousand Kurds were annihilated.

In early 1988, Saddam Hussein categorized the Kurds with the Iranians when he declared war on Iran. Hussein ruthlessly killed men, women, and children with sarin and mustard gas. Nearly 5,000 people were killed in the attack.[84] The Turks also have a history of persecuting and purging the Kurds.

The Kurds' relationship with the United States is rocky, as well. The United States has an unforgiving and embarrassing history of breaking promises to the Kurds and abandoning them; and the Kurds have a long history of hurt to demand revenge for. But I know of some Kurds who would not desire to seek revenge because something interesting happened to change their outlook.

On October 2, 2006, a crazed gunman walked into a one-room schoolhouse in an Amish community in Nickel Mines, Pennsylvania. The gunman, Charles Roberts IV, took hostages and shot ten girls between the ages of six and thirteen before committing suicide.

Jonas Stoltzfus' family was among the many members of the Amish community broken by the tragedy. When I met with him, he told me about the event. "My oldest sister had three daughters that were in the school during the shooting that day. The oldest daughter was killed, another was wounded, and one ran out through a side door of the building and survived."

Shortly after this shooting, several thousand miles away, some Kurds in Iraq watched the events unfold on television, and they were deeply moved by the forgiveness that the Amish showered upon the killer and his family. Instead of seeking revenge, the Amish community members came together and showed love both to one another and to the gunman.

These Kurds in Iraq were amazed by the Amish community that, through forgiveness, healed their own hurt, pain, and loss.

As we shared a Chinese meal in Topeka, Kansas, in 2014, Jonas Stoltzfus said, "We were hit hard by it all, but God's grace was all that we knew to heal the pain."

The Kurds with government connections contacted members of the Amish community and begged them to send representatives to Iraq to teach them about the kind of forgiveness that they had displayed.

Two of the representatives who were sent from the Amish community were Steve and Jake Lapp, who are known as the Lapp brothers. Steve and Jake traveled to northern Iraq to teach the Kurds about the forgiveness of Jesus Christ.

Through that tragic event, a relationship was formed that showed the power of prayer and forgiveness. The Kurds could not find anything in the Koran that taught the same kind of biblical prayer and forgiveness exhibited by the Amish. They had searched the Koran and had come up empty-handed.

After ISIS attacked the Kurdish villages in Syria and Iraq, the Lapp brothers were invited back to Iraq. Steve and Jake knew that they had to return and again share the love, forgiveness, and reconciliation that only Christ can give. It was the best way that the Kurds knew to deal with the ISIS crisis, because ISIS is united by bitterness and hatred. If the hatred and bitterness were removed, ISIS would fall apart.

On September 8, 2014, the Lapp brothers traveled to Iraq. Their trip came shortly after ISIS took Mosul and beheaded James Foley. September was right in the middle of the most intense time, when the refugees were still fleeing and persecution was at its peak.

"God told us to go to Nineveh, which is Mosul, and to pray against that Nimrod spirit," Steve Lapp said to me. "God told us to put boots on the ground."

The Lapp brothers believe that God gave them a mandate to go and pray over the situation in Kurdistan, and they hope to see this Iraqi minority people group supported through the prayers of Christian believers. The Kurdish military appreciate the devotion of the Amish community to their people, and they welcomed the Lapp brothers with open arms.

"We were taken by [Kurdish] military escort to the mountain overlooking Nineveh to pray," Steve said, remembering the day they were taken to the highest point.

"Only a few days prior to that, ISIS had controlled that mountain," said Jake.

"So, we were on top of the mountain, looking down into the valley," Steve continued, "and at the bottom of the mountain was a village that ISIS was in control of when we were praying. We were standing there in the 'high place,' and they were telling us to be careful, because, you know, there is always the possibility of a sniper picking you off right where you are. But we believed that we were to stand here in this high place and pray."

Steve recalled the events of the story in his Pennsylvania-Dutch accent as closely as he could. As he talked, I looked at some of the pictures that he had taken with his iPhone. He was not exaggerating. He was on top of a mountain ridge with a military escort, which was made up of four SUVs and at least ten soldiers. All of the soldiers were practicing caution on the mountain, but Steve and his brother, Jake, were standing upright, praying over the ISIS camps below. They were not wearing helmets or bulletproof vests; they were dressed in their Amish clothing from Lancaster, Pennsylvania, which, oddly enough, fit in well with the simple, earth-toned clothing that many of the rural Kurds wear.

It seemed odd to me that Steve and Jake were given a military escort. They were not military strategists. To a logical person, the four SUVs and the fuel to drive them could have been better used to carry equipment in battle with ISIS. The military personnel escorting them could have been better used on the frontlines. Taking a couple of country Amish guys from America to a mountain could not have been a bigger waste of time and resources, especially when you consider that the Amish are pacifists; they do not even believe in war.

Steve explained why he was there with his brother risking his life in Iraq. "We believe we are not to fight in the natural realm because we do not wrestle with flesh and blood. But, in the spirit realm, we are very militant, because we believe that prayer changes things. We believe that the weapons of warfare are not carnal, but that they are mighty through God for the purpose of pulling down strongholds. If we do not wrestle with flesh and blood but with principalities and powers and rulers of darkness and spiritual wickedness in high places, then why are we not doing our job so that the military doesn't have to?"

Jake jumped in to follow up. "And you know what is interesting? The next day, the [Kurdish] military in that area where we had just prayed took back seven villages."

Compare the approach of the prayers of the Lapp brothers to that of the U.S.-led bombing campaign that started around the same time. During the initial stages of the campaign, ISIS actually advanced and took new territory, but it was not Kurdish lands, home of those who took the time to pray. It seems that the Kurds are learning something about the power of prayer, and things are changing for their land.

The fight in Syria has given ISIS momentum on the battlefield and catapulted its efforts in Iraq. With the U.S. pullout, Iraq has found itself in a fragile situation, and ISIS has flowed in to fill in the vacuum. The United States and her Western allies are not eager to return to the Iraqi battle theater.

Because of ISIS, the tables have turned for the Kurds in Iraq. The unthinkable has happened. Western countries have backed the rebels in the fight against the Syrian government, unwittingly helping

ISIS to achieve its objective. Now, Syria is unstable, ISIS has the upper hand, and the West watches helplessly as the situation unfolds.

Only the Kurds have shown the resolve and the determination to fight back against ISIS. They also seem to be the only ones crazy enough to invest their resources in the power of prayer.

The Battle for Kirkuk, Iraq

After capturing Mosul, ISIS decided to move on to Kirkuk, Iraq, on the southern border of Kurdistan. When it saw what had happened in Mosul, the Iraqi Army lost its resolve to fight, and the army of several thousand dissolved in hours. ISIS took town after town with very little resistance. Militants took over outposts with little more than two-bit terrorists in taxicabs and pickup trucks. When the Iraqi Army went into full retreat mode, Kirkuk fell into the hands of ISIS.

The Kurdish leadership saw the city in the hands of ISIS and mobilized peshmerga fighters to take the city back. Within hours of moving in, the Kurds seized full control of Kirkuk.

Now the American leadership is siding with the Iraqis and demanding that the Kurds do two impossible acts: first, risk the lives of their young men to fight and kill ISIS jihadists without the aid of the Iraqi military or American financial support; second, remain under the control of the Iraqi government.

Again, the Kurds have always been loyal to America. Their loyalty could not be seen more than during the most recent Iraqi war. From 2003, when the United States invaded Iraq, until its pullout almost ten years later, there was not even one American soldier who died in the Kurdish-controlled area of Iraq.

The Kurds have devoted themselves to the cause of other nations for so long, but now they are working toward fulfilling their national dream to taste independence. They have waited such a long time for this opportunity.

The problem with an official Kurdistan is that it will come only at the end of the nightmare of ISIS, and it will begin a new nightmare for all the surrounding Islamic countries.

SEVEN

The ISIS Threat

"My brother and I are very close," said Zybandeh Abedini, whose friends call her "ZZ." She was speaking to me about her older brother, Saeed Abedini, an Iranian-born pastor who is in prison in Iran. We did not know it then, but Pastor Saeed Abedini would become one of ISIS's major targets because of his faith in Jesus Christ.

ZZ and I were sitting together in a cabin in the Smoky Mountains, Pigeon Forge, Tennessee, when she opened up about the sensitive situation involving her brother. At the time, Pastor Saeed's predicament in Iran was being watched by the entire world.

Pastor Saeed Abedini

During the 2014 National Prayer Breakfast in the United States, President Barack Obama said,

> We pray for Pastor Saeed Abedini. He's been held in Iran for more than 18 months, sentenced to eight years in prison on charges relating to his Christian beliefs....And as we continue to work on his freedom, today, again, we

> call on the Iranian government to release Pastor Abedini so he can return to the loving arms of his wife and children in Idaho.[85]

ZZ had flown to Tennessee to join me for a special Back to Jerusalem (BTJ) ambassador meeting. BTJ ambassadors go around the United States and share the vision of the Chinese underground church. ZZ had wanted to be a part of the meeting, and she had volunteered to teach the Persian language to the BTJ Chinese missionaries who were moving to Iran.

"Our relationship was always close," ZZ continued, "so I remember when my brother started to act differently. I went into his room and looked around, wondering why he was acting so different. In his room, I found a Bible."

ZZ was very surprised by her discovery. Their father worked for the Islamic Iranian government, and their mother was a very conservative orthodox Muslim. Bibles were not allowed in their home; they were not allowed in any Iranian Muslim home. If the Bible were found in their house, the entire family would be in danger. ZZ was immediately curious about what was going on with her brother, and she wondered if the Bible had anything to do with the changes she had seen in him.

Saeed had always been loving and kind toward his baby sister Zybandeh, but he'd had a dark side to him—he'd hated Christians and everything they represented. His zeal and passion for Islam had been recognized by those around him. As a young man, he'd been approached by Hezbollah and recruited to be a suicide bomber.

A Christian church not far from their home had consumed Saeed's thoughts. He'd wanted to kill the pastor for the lies that he taught; but that had all changed, and ZZ didn't know why.

Curious, she asked her brother about it when they were out by themselves. "I found a Bible in your room. What happened? Why is that Bible in your room?"

"Do you want to know what has happened to me?" Saeed asked, knowing that he could trust her to keep such a dangerous secret. He began telling the amazing story about how Jesus had appeared to him.

At a nearby park, he'd heard the gospel from a young man who eventually became one of his best friends. Later, he'd heard a pastor saying that Jesus is God. Saeed had always acknowledged that Jesus was a prophet, as the Koran teaches; but to believe that He was God had seemed blasphemous and had angered him.

"I didn't believe that Jesus was God. What were they talking about? These were lies. These Christians were lying to these people. I told myself that I would kill that pastor one day because he was a liar," Saeed told ZZ.

Saeed went on to tell his sister how he'd eventually begun to read both the Koran and the Bible and had compared the two. He had been so confused. One day, he'd prayed, "Allah, if Islam is the true religion, show me. Show me something. The Christian people say that God talks to them. Why are you not talking to me?"

Saeed continued, "That same night, I had a vision in my dream. Jesus appeared to me. He said, 'Saeed, I am coming. Evangelize My name.' When I woke up, I didn't know if it had been real or not. I thought it was because I was thinking about this kind of stuff."

He had gone back to sleep, and again Jesus had said to him, "Saeed, I am coming back. Evangelize My name."

"The third time was so powerful," Saeed said. "Again, I was told to go and evangelize, but, this time, I could see Jesus leaving my room. My body was shaking." Immediately, Saeed had repented of his sins and committed his life to follow Christ.

These events occurred in 2000. Soon afterward, Saeed's entire family came to Christ, and he began to plant underground churches throughout the country.

Thirteen years later, I woke up to an e-mail from Paul Hattaway, a man I have worked with for years. Paul is a respected Christian author from New Zealand who is passionate about the Back to Jerusalem vision. Many know him as the coauthor of the acclaimed book *The Heavenly Man*, a testimony of Brother Yun. Paul does not often send e-mails to me requesting prayer, so this one caught my attention.

> A dear personal friend of mine is in trouble for no reason except that he loves and obeys Jesus Christ. His name is Saeed Abedini. He was born in Iran but is now a U.S. citizen. His wife, Naghmeh, is also a U.S. citizen, and they live with their two children in the U.S. state of Idaho.
>
> Saeed, despite being just 32 years old, has been instrumental in bringing many Iranian Muslims to the Lord, and has established numerous house churches throughout Iran.
>
> He asked me to write his biography, and I was working on it when Saeed made one last trip back to Iran.
>
> In September of last year, Saeed was traveling on a bus near the Iranian border when revolutionary guards boarded the bus and dragged him off. He was held for months while he waited for his case to come before the courts of Iran. He is currently held captive in the notorious Evin Prison in Tehran. He has been mercilessly tortured but has not denied his Lord and Savior.

After being detained for questioning by the revolutionary guard, Saeed was put under house arrest until September 26, 2012, when he was taken away from his mother's home in chains. During his incarceration in Evin Prison, he endured solitary confinement, beatings and other physical torture, and internal bleeding.

"He is being tortured because he will not deny his faith," his wife, Naghmeh, told me at a Starbucks coffee shop in Boise, Idaho, during a brief meeting in 2014.

"What are they actually accusing him of? Are they saying that he did something against the government?" I asked her.

"According to the court, his work in Christian churches from 2000 to 2005 was a threat to the security of Iran," she replied. "In 2009, we were assured by the Iranian Intelligence Ministry that he could travel to Iran without any problems if we agreed to work on humanitarian efforts and stay clear of the churches. My husband agreed not to be an active pastor and instead to focus on helping Iranian orphans by building an orphanage. He sought to help the fatherless of Iran, and now Iran is taking away my children's father."

Naghmeh was remarkably strong and confident. She continued, "Saeed always had a heart for the Chinese and the Back to Jerusalem vision. He even traveled to Germany to meet with Brother Yun after he had read *The Heavenly Man*." She paused for a moment. "I also have the same feeling [about the Chinese missionaries]. I really like the way that the Chinese focus on preaching the gospel in the closed countries. I had a vision of me being on a plane. I was flying to Iran, and, when I looked around, I noticed that everyone else who was on the plane was not Iranian. They were Chinese. I could see that they were all wearing rice hats, like the ones you see in the movies, and we were all flying together to Iran."

In November 2013, ZZ sent me a message asking us to pray. Saeed had been transferred in the middle of the night out of Evin Prison. Eventually, we learned that he had been moved to the dreaded Rajai-Shahr Prison in Karaj, Iran, also known as Gohardasht Prison, where prisoners go to disappear.

Prisoners who are considered to be a headache for the government are placed in Rajai-Shahr, where the most violent prisoners are held. If a few of the prisoners kill each other, it is actually considered a favor to the government.

Rajai-Shahr Prison is overcrowded and full of dangerous convicted murderers, rapists, drug addicts, and terrorists, including terrorists linked to ISIS. Most prisoners at Rajai-Shahr have no hope of ever getting out and have very little to lose. Many of them see ISIS as a band of heroes; so, when ISIS issued a threat to have Pastor Saeed killed, they took it very seriously.

"This is an extremely dangerous development that puts Pastor Saeed's life at grave risk," said Jay Sekulow, chief counsel of the American Center for Law and Justice (ACLJ). "Not only is Pastor Saeed facing threats from Iranian militants who have imprisoned him because of his Christian faith, he now faces new and perhaps even more dangerous threats from Iraqi ISIS prisoners who want to murder Pastor Saeed because of his faith."[86]

The caliph al-Baghdadi has a special connection to hardened criminals. Because he spent time in prison, he identifies with them. He aims to empower them, set them free, and add them to the ranks of his followers.

Soon after ISIS took control of Mosul, they stormed the nearest correctional facility, Badush Prison. Arriving there, they found the place free of guards. Knowing that ISIS was coming, the guards had run away during the night.

At the prison, the ISIS gunmen were immediately greeted by hungry and thirsty inmates who had been abandoned in their cells. ISIS separated the Sunni prisoners from all the other inmates. The Shias, Christians, and Yazidis were separated into other groups.[87]

ISIS jihadists then took the Sunnis and methodically questioned them to make sure there were no posers trying to escape punishment. Prisoners around the Muslim-believing world noted that the Sunni prisoners were set free and given the chance to be a part of something larger than they are.

To many Muslim jihadists who are rotting away in prison, joining ISIS has been like being born again. They are ready and willing to serve the terrorist group, obeying whatever is asked of them. When Pastor Saeed learned that the command to kill him had been given, he had to act quickly. He imposed solitary confinement on himself, because ISIS members in the prison yard were ready to carry out the orders.

Support for ISIS is growing globally, and its influence continues to increase. As it grows, the number of Christian leaders who will be killed or threatened like Pastor Saeed will also increase. Although the initial focus of ISIS was to take over Iraq and Syria, it has also wielded its power and influence in Iran, as seen in the situation with Pastor Saeed.

As of the writing of this book, Pastor Saeed has been in prison for two years, separated from his wife and two young children, who live in Boise, Idaho, as well as his younger sister ZZ. His immediate family members living in Iran are able to visit him on a regular basis, but their visits are often cut short because of Pastor Saeed's poor physical condition from enduring so many beatings.

In spite of all of the persecution, Pastor Saeed refuses to deny the name of his Savior Jesus Christ. From his prison cell, he wrote,

> Prison is a test of faith. I was always worried that the storms of life would break the ship of [my] faith, but when you stand in the steadfast ship of faith, the storms are like a nice breeze. Nothing can break the ship of faith. These walls have created more fervor for me to love others

> through sharing the Gospel, but more than that, the walls have deepened my love for my Savior. I feel the prayers of all who are praying for me. I hope to one day meet each one of them face to face and embrace them in my arms.[88]

The government of Iran has not been able to make Pastor Saeed recant his faith, and there is no evidence that would lead us to believe that ISIS will be any more successful.

At the 2015 National Prayer Breakfast, President Obama gave an update about Pastor Saeed, explaining that he had received an "extraordinary" letter from him and saying, "He describes his captivity and expressed his gratitude for my visit with his family and thanked us all for standing in solidarity with him during his captivity." The letter included the following statement: "Nothing is more valuable to the Body of Christ than to see how the Lord is in control and moves ahead of countries and leadership through united prayer." Pastor Saeed referred to himself as a "prisoner for Christ who is proud to be part of this great nation, the United States of America that cares for religious freedom across the world." Obama concluded, "We're going to keep up this work for Pastor Abedini and all those around the world who are unjustly held or persecuted because of their faith."[89]

The Yazidi People

Prior to the most recent crisis in Iraq with ISIS, most people had never heard of the Yazidi people. Their existence has become known throughout the world because of the unusual persecution they have been enduring at the hands of ISIS. Even so, there is still much to learn about them.

Christians, Jews, Kurds, and Shia Muslims have also been persecuted and attacked, but all have a certain amount of assistance. Iraqi Christians have solidarity with those in the world community who share their faith. There are very few Jews left in Iraq today due to the Jewish migration to Israel following World War II. And the Shia Muslims have a claim in the Iraqi government, as well as friends across the border in Iran. The Kurds are solidified in their dream of one day having their own homeland; and, as mentioned in the previous chapter, peshmerga forces have been remarkably successful in repelling the attacks of ISIS. In contrast to the above-mentioned groups, the Yazidis have no such connections or resources.

The Yazidis are a small minority group with a population of roughly 700,000 who live primarily in the northern region of Iraq. While they are considered mysterious to the rest of the world, they are despised by ISIS, as well as by most other Muslims. They have been hunted down like rabbits by jihadists who find joy in terrorizing the weak. Indeed, the weakness of the Yazidi people has made them primary targets of ISIS.

At first glance, many people mistakenly think that the Yazidis are Sunni Kurds. Yazidis are noted more for the distinctiveness of their religion than for the distinctiveness of their clothing, comparable to how it is among Chinese minority tribes.

The Yazidi people have lived in the mountains of northern Iraq for generations. It is home to all the places they hold sacred. All of the main shrines, storied villages, and holy places are in the province of Nineveh, which is now the front line of the fight with ISIS. Furthermore, every year, Yazidis make pilgrimages to the holy city of Lalish just outside of Mosul.

Similar to the social practices among the people groups of India, the Yazidis have a caste system, and intermarrying is forbidden among the different castes. Because the Yazidi population is not very large, young people are forced to marry their cousins and second cousins.

Religious Beliefs

Not much is really known or understood about the Yazidi religion, because, for their own protection, the Yazidis have kept much of it hidden from the Muslims, who are in the majority in Iraq. One cannot convert to the Yazidi religion; one must be born into it.

Only certain clergy members of the priestly caste fully understand the religious practices and traditions of the Yazidis. The religion borrows heavily from Islam, Christianity, and Judaism, and shares many tenets of the Zoroastrian faith, which, historically, is from neighboring Iran. Like the local Muslims, Yazidis refrain from eating certain foods, such as pork, and they also practice male circumcision. But unlike the Muslims, the Yazidis face the sun when they pray—not Mecca. This infuriates orthodox Muslims. Another tradition that makes the Yazidis noticeably different from other groups is that they recognize Wednesday as their holy day and Saturday as their day of rest.

Yazidis are often misunderstood because they do not fit into any particular religion. They have a rich tradition, but because they have no unified written religious code, they lack the kind of systematic theology that is found in Islam and Christianity.

The Yazidi religion relies heavily on oral tradition and strict adherence to cultural customs. Yazidis are monotheistic, but they believe that God has left seven angels, or holy beings, to be in charge of His creation. The supreme holy being is also known as the peacock angel, which Muslims consider to be equivalent to Satan. The Islamic experience with the Satanic Verses that were given to Muhammad makes them reject everything that the Yazidi believe about the peacock angel.

The Yazidis are able to relate to a few Christian teachings. For example, they believe that there was once a man named Jesus. To them, Christ was a heavenly being who took on the form of man. And, like the Christians and the Jews, the Yazidis believe in Adam and Eve; but, oddly, they believe that they descend only from Adam and have no relation to Eve.

It is this mix of religious ideology that makes it difficult to understand them—especially, it seems, for members of ISIS. That is why, as the Islamic State continues to persecute them, Yazidis find themselves at the receiving end of a special kind of persecution. "Our entire religion is being wiped off the face of the earth," said Yazidi leader Vian Dakhil.[90]

Persecution

The year 2014 will likely go down in history as one of the most difficult times for the Yazidi people. In August 2014, ISIS attacked many of the villages in northern Iraq where this people group lived. In anticipation of this attack, most of the people fled their homes and ran to the mountains in order to survive. But what kind of "survival" are they now experiencing? Many Yazidis who escaped have to live with the memory of their sons and daughters being ripped from their arms. Or of their children dying of dehydration as exiles. Some survivors have to carry the mental image of their mothers and fathers being executed. They can only imagine what it was like for those who did not escape.

Yet the Yazidis who were fortunate enough to make it to the safety of the mountains did not have shelter from the sun during the day or a bed to lie on at night. They found that a new enemy—starvation—was waiting for them around the corner, and they were forced to eat leaves and grass to stay alive. On the rare occasion when they found an animal to consume for protein, they had to eat it raw, having no way to cook it.

While many of the Yazidis escaped, ISIS apprehended a number of Yazidis who did not have anywhere to run or hide. Several Yazidi villages were captured, and the terrorists attempted to systematically force the people to convert to Islam. Almost all the captives rejected the Islamic faith, and an estimated 500 of them were killed, including men, women, and children, while others were buried alive.[91] Those whom ISIS captured but did not kill were introduced to a most evil side of humanity.

Yazidi Women Forced into Sex Slavery

Yazidi women reported to officials that the younger Yazidi girls were handpicked by ISIS fighters and forcefully married. Others were sold as sex slaves. One fifteen-year-old girl who escaped captivity and who goes by the alias Rewshe said that she, her sister, and two hundred other women were held for three weeks and taken to an ISIS-controlled city in Syria. The day after they arrived in Syria, she was sold to a Palestinian ISIS fighter for $1,000 (U.S.). Her sister was sold to another ISIS fighter.[92]

One eye witness said that she had seen girls as young as twelve and thirteen being sold. Other girls were given in forced marriage to ISIS fighters as prizes.[93]

During an interview with BBC World Service, a man named Karam shared stories of Yazidi women who were taken by ISIS. He recalled his phone conversation with a young, scared Yazidi girl who had been ripped from her family and forced to serve as a sex slave.

The woman had begged, "If you know where we are, please bomb us.... There is no life after this. I am going to kill myself anyway—others have killed themselves this morning." She was desperate and crying. Death was her only hope; after enduring the sexual punishment of the jihadists, she felt that life was not worth living. Karam recalled her saying, "I have been raped thirty times, and it's not even lunch time. I can't go to the toilet. Please bomb us."[94]

The UN has compared the slaughter of the Yazidi people to the Bosnian Srebrenica massacre. Furthermore, researchers piecing together various reports of the attacks on Yazidis have concluded that 5,000 of this people group have been gunned down in a series of attacks, and at least 5,000–7,000 Yazidi women are being held in detention centers from which they will be sold into slavery or handed over as sex slaves. There are an estimated 3,500 women and children being held captive in five detention centers in Tal Afar, Iraq.[95]

ISIS has released videos of training camps full of young boys as young as five years old pledging allegiance to the Islamic State. Video footage in Iraq has shown young boys at school lined up in military formation, preparing to take jihadist exams. Young children were holding AK-47s. All of them came from families that live in the newly conquered territories.

Today, the majority of Yazidis have been displaced by ISIS. After having been forced to leave their homes, they are now living in abandoned buildings and temporary tents. They do not know what tomorrow will bring. Though Kurds are often accused of not liking Yazidis, they are the only thing now standing between the Yazidis and the Islamic State.

Yazidi Refugees

While working in the Yazidi refugee camps in northern Iraq, I was able to meet with Dr. Paul Kingery, director of the Displacements and Migration Center at American University in Dohuk, Iraq. Dr. Paul is one of the few allies of the Yazidi people, and an unsung hero of their cause. He is also one of the most highly respected authorities working with refugees of ISIS in northern Iraq, and he told me, "You know, the Yazidis are considered dirty by the Kurds. No one wants to live beside them. They are not really welcomed in some of the villages because of this false idea that they do not bathe. It is just not true! They do bathe; they just do not bathe on Wednesday because of their religious beliefs. They also do not have access to water. It is really difficult to keep clean when you do not have water."

Dr. Paul is the main coordinator of the various NGOs (nongovernmental organizations) that have come to help with the refugee crisis in Iraq, and he is, in many ways, a one-man crusade. As a key player for the newly established American University, Dr. Paul's hands are full, but he has put his life and career on hold to spearhead the effort to help the refugees of ISIS, specifically the Yazidi people.

In early November 2014, Dr. Paul was asked to join a meeting with the presidents of Kurdistan and Iraq. His extensive knowledge of the area and his dedication to the displaced people are inspiring to everyone who has the pleasure of meeting with him.

Dr. Paul has adopted a village just north of Mosul where many of the refugees have fled. "We need to really pull together to help these people. If we do not, no one else will. The Christians are helping the Christians, the Muslims are helping the Muslims, the Kurds are helping the Kurds, but no one is really helping the Yazidi people."

Unlike the UN's efforts to provide tent cities in mud-filled fields, Dr. Paul has worked hard to secure brick-and-mortar housing in which the Yazidis can live long-term. At the time of this writing, all the housing was not yet completed, but as many as 4,000 to 5,000 Yazidis are now living in homes that provide shelter from the cold weather and rain.

One sunny morning in November 2014, Dr. Paul and I sat in the back of an old beige Toyota taxi on our way to meet with one of the Yazidi village leaders. Dr. Paul pulled out a manila envelope and removed a picture of a completed house that he had been working on. "This is the design that we have for our homes in the area. The

Yazidis are not going to be allowed to stay here for long. We already had the first case of a refugee family being evicted, but I am going to submit a plan to the leader of the village that will allow them to collect money for the housing, as well as allow the Yazidi to stay."

As I walked through the village in which Dr. Paul had been working, I met many of the families that had escaped death. Standing in the doorway of one of the gray brick buildings was a man with a long, black, cotton trench coat. He waved at us, and I waved back. He was so excited to see a new visitor in the village.

"Hello, how are you?" he asked with a heavy accent. He was a large, imposing Yazidi man with a thick beard. He came over and grabbed my hand to shake it. His handshake was strong enough to move my entire body. He had the kind of solid strength that comes from hard work and age, which is often called "old man strength."

A translator relayed his next question: "Where are you from?" He had expended all of his English, and I lacked any Kurdish or Yazidi vocabulary.

"America," he answered, before I said a word.

I nodded my head yes.

"I used to be in the army," he said right away. "I worked with the Americans. Do you know David? David in the American army?" He enthusiastically nodded his head at us as if he expected us to know exactly who David was.

"David is from California. He is my friend. He calls me." He was so proud of his relationship with the American. It must have been one of the few things that kept his mind from thinking back on the recent nightmare perpetrated by ISIS.

This man was a major target for the terrorist group, for three reasons: he was Yazidi, he served in the Iraqi Army, and he cooperated with the U.S. military.

"How many people live in your house?" I asked, pointing to his home, where a crowd had started to form at the doorway.

He held up three fingers.

"Three people?" I asked.

"Three families," he replied.

"Here comes my brother," he said, waving to him to come and join us.

In his arms, the brother held a small baby, whom he handed over to his brother. The strong Yazidi man gently took the baby and cradled him. He was such a large, hairy, burly man, and he had just engaged in face-to-face combat with ISIS in order to help his family escape. However, in an instant, with the baby in his arms, he turned into a softer version of himself, like a docile teddy bear.

"This baby was born in the mountains when ISIS was chasing after us," he said. His sister had had no choice but to run to the mountainside seeking shelter when she was nine months pregnant. It had not been easy for her to navigate the rocky mountainside, but she'd needed to do it to protect her unborn child. Her brother had carried two of the family's little girls, one in each arm, as he led the way.

"We did not have food for two weeks. No water. I had to walk for miles to get only a little water for our family."

After just a few days in the mountains, his sister had gone into labor. She'd had none of the comforts of having a baby in a hospital, but she had given birth on the rocks to a very healthy baby boy. Not even ISIS had been able to stop the power of new life.

It wasn't an uncommon story in the Yazidi village. Every person had a horror story of what happened to him or her when ISIS attacked the village.

One refugee, known as Shamo, told the Christian news group CBN that he had been trapped in the mountains for eight days and had seen ISIS kill 170 Yazidi men, then take their wives and daughters to sell as slaves. Like most Yazidis, Shamo wanted nothing to do with Islam because of ISIS and the atrocities committed by Muslims he had once considered friends. Shamo left the Yazidi faith and became a believer in Jesus Christ.[96]

Here is the gripping account of what happened to a young man who survived a different attack by ISIS. Thirteen-year-old Solomon was awakened from his sleep. Concrete chunks propelled through the air, and plumes of smoke filled his room. Something had exploded.

"I jumped out of bed, ran down to the kitchen, and saw that my house was being bombed. A small piece of shrapnel hit me on the shoulder. The second floor where my room was located was being destroyed by the continual bombing."

Bombs were going off all around. He could hear his neighbors screaming.

"We ran out of the house and tried to escape the village. All of the children in my family were crying. We were all scared and did not know what was happening or where to run. Bombs were dropping beside us and shaking the ground."

The debris from the blasts was flying everywhere.

"We tried to find a safe place to hide, but there was nowhere to go. We were afraid that if we stayed in one location, we would be killed, and if we continued to run, we would be killed. There was no place to go where we could hide from the bombing."

"All around us, we could see dead bodies, body parts, and even people who had been decapitated from the explosions."

After about thirty minutes to an hour, the bombing stopped. Solomon's family ran back to their house, which had been mostly destroyed. His parents quickly searched through the debris to find their IDs and some other necessities. In just a few minutes, they had to choose what to bring. They grabbed some extra clothing and ran to the next village. Nobody was certain what had happened. It was extremely confusing.

"Not long afterward, a truck came around, and I was recruited to help pick up the dead people and body parts, and throw them into the back of the truck."

But the violence wasn't over yet. The jihadists had only prepared the way with the bombing, which had been intended to weaken the village in order to give the terrorists a greater advantage for their attack. They drove in on trucks and shot people, even women and children. People fell down and died. There was mass chaos everywhere—confusion about which direction to go.

In the end, the entire village was destroyed. Solomon's school had been bombed. Those who survived began a vagabond life on the run.

"I have seven sisters and one baby brother who needed to be rushed out. We went to Halibo, which is a several hours' walking distance from my village. We got in our car and drove to town, where we were able to stay with our uncle. Work was not easy to find, so we did everything we could to land a job. I worked to get money for my family."

Solomon found a job at a small restaurant. One day, on his way to work, he was stopped at a checkpoint. When the guards searched him, they found a small knife that he kept in his pocket for his job at the restaurant. He used it to peel vegetables when he wasn't waiting on tables, and he had totally forgotten that he had it in his pocket.

When the guards saw the knife, they told Solomon, "You have to come with us."

Solomon thought that he was in trouble for carrying the knife, and he promised them that he did not want to use the knife to hurt anyone. They told him they did not intend to punish him for the crime, but they needed him to serve in the local military to fight ISIS.

He was taken to meet some military leaders. "I pleaded with them and told them that I was too small to fight, but they refused to listen to me and yelled at me to shut up. My mother and father were not there. I was in a room full of older military men who had more authority than my parents." Solomon was a refugee, and his words did not mean much.

"They wrote down my name and told me that I had to serve in the Syrian Army. I was drafted to serve as a soldier."

Soon, Solomon was issued a rifle and taught how to shoot it, clean it, and maintain it.

"My Syrian Army instructor looked at me and told me very clearly that if I did not kill ISIS, he would kill me. I was sent out to fight ISIS."

"When our unit was engaged in a small skirmish, I didn't see anyone. I was scared and did not want to kill anyone, so I closed my eyes and shot my weapon until I ran out of bullets. I was so relieved that I did not have any more bullets. That provided me with an excuse to not fight any more and to not kill anyone."

However, when Solomon's commander saw that he had run out of ammunition, he gave him more. He could probably sense that he was scared. "Fight!" he yelled at Solomon. "The more you fight, and the more people you kill, the easier it will become. You will get tougher with each shot," he said.

Solomon continued, "After I was recruited, ISIS affiliates had set up a checkpoint to locate soldiers. Soldiers were killed immediately on site upon discovery. I was able to find a way around the checkpoint. I strapped my weapon to my back and ran into an urban area. I found a big apartment building and ran inside and up the stairs. On the roof of the building was a water tank. The opening was large enough for me to climb inside. It was only half-filled with water, because ISIS had turned the water off to the city before the fighting had begun."

With the skirmish still going on, Solomon felt that the water tank looked like a great place to hide. He crawled down inside with his rifle in hand. He pulled the lid closed above his head and sat there alone in the dark with his rifle pointed at the small opening.

"I told myself that if anyone opened the lid, I would shoot them."

Solomon's shoulder was still bleeding from the injury he'd sustained at the bombing of his home. It was taking a long time to heal. During the skirmish, the wound had reopened, and blood was flowing into the water tank.

After he had spent several hours in the tank, the shooting stopped. There was a lull in the battle. "I opened up the water tank, peered over the roof, and saw people running away. I threw down my gun and ran out of the house to join the crowds."

Solomon was not wearing a soldier's uniform, so he looked like any other boy running with his family away from the village. He boarded a bus with the refugees and traveled alone to Iraq, where another uncle lived.

Solomon did not have a passport or travel papers with him. "I was stopped at the checkpoint and asked for my papers, but I told them that our family had been attacked." There were many refugees crossing the border at that time.

"Why are you going to Iraq?" they asked. "Why are you leaving your country?"

After some time, Solomon was allowed to cross into Iraq. Soon after entering, he experienced more troubles. He found out that ISIS was just outside of Dohuk, where he was living. His mother and seven sisters were living in a Syrian refugee camp. His father had found an open door to get into Germany and had taken Solomon's baby brother with him to see if he could establish a new life in Europe and have his family rejoin him later. Yet there was no guarantee that would happen any day soon.

The German government has tightened its immigration policy. We have seen that Brother Yun travels on refugee papers that have been issued by the German government. Because he is considered to be a persecuted Christian pastor, Brother Yun has been granted residency by the German government. His children have grown up in Germany and have gone through the German school system. They are now Germans, but Brother Yun and his wife still have not been able to obtain German citizenship.

If Solomon, his mother, and his siblings put all their hope in the idea of their father coming back to Iraq to take them to a better life in Germany, their wait may be long. The process could take years. In the meantime, all the needs of Solomon's family rest on him; at this time, he is still only sixteen years old.

Solomon has been taken in and adopted by an American, who has provided him with an education, as well as an opportunity to make money. Solomon works hard to help his family survive, but he also helps other Syrian refugees whose needs are like those of his own family.

When I sat down with Solomon to talk about his story, he was remarkably strong. The graphic memories of dead bodies and war that remain in his mind would make most people go insane, but Solomon has found strength in Jesus Christ.

When I see this young man, I think of my oldest son, who is only one year younger than he. I imagine my son waking up in his room as it is being blasted by bombs, and not knowing what to do or where to go. I visualize him running through the streets of a war zone and being captured and forced to serve in an impromptu militia.

Solomon should be able to spend his afternoons with friends after school. He should be worried only about his next exam, not about whether he is going to live or die. He is still a youth, but he is being forced into manhood. His innocence has been robbed from him.

"I do not like Islam," Solomon once said when we were riding together in a taxi. "Kill, kill, kill. This is all I see from this religion."

I remained silent. I knew that Solomon was speaking from his own experience.

"Are you a Christian?" I eventually asked.

"I go to church," he responded.

I wanted to say that going to church and following Jesus were not the same thing, but I understood his point.

"Sometimes, I go to church just to feel peace," he said. "I can feel love and peace at church. Christians help people—that is good."

To Solomon, the difference between Jesus and Muhammad is not a small one.

There are many Solomons scattered around the desert mountains of Syria, Iraq, and Turkey, but there were many boys who did not escape their rooms when the bombs came raining down. There are other boys who were not able to find a water tank to hide in to escape the army that had forcefully drafted them. There are boys who were not so fortunate as to find a loving American Christian who would adopt them into his family.

And it is not just the Syrian militia that drafts mere boys as recruits for fighting. ISIS forces many young boys in its camps to fight. It is brainwashing them and abusing them. It is creating Islamic soldiers who will give their lives in jihad.

Many of these young men are now ready to give their life for this cause. The only way to reach them is through an equal amount of dedication and self-sacrifice.

EIGHT

ISIS, the PLO, Hezbollah, and Hamas

As mentioned previously, ISIS initially set its sights on conquering Iraq and Syria, ergo its name. It has succeeded in overtaking about half of each country. Iraq and Syria both have fertile lands, arid deserts, and jagged mountain ranges. Rivers that once met the needs of the earliest civilizations on earth flow through these two countries, and the bones of leaders who led the most powerful empires of their time are buried here.

Large numbers of refugees have fled to Turkey from both Iraq and Syria, in hopes of getting away from ISIS. Though they are finding safety in the Kurdish-controlled areas of Iraq and Syria, many feel even safer in Turkey. The refugees are very confident that the advancement of ISIS will stop at the Turkish border.

Even if ISIS is not successful in moving into Turkey or conquering more territory in the near future, many people acknowledge that going into their camps and conquering them seems more and more like a distant dream. So many coalition countries are fatigued from battle and seem to be content with a "wait and see" approach. But if the world waits any longer, it might resign itself to seeing a new country established—the Islamic State. At this time, it does not seem as if ISIS is making any additional aggressive advancements, but it very well may be digging in and developing its own type of government, as it has always wanted.

As scary as it is to think about, it seems as if ISIS is becoming a "normal" country. Of course, it is not normal to a Western citizen, but it is normal in that the world is slowly getting used to the idea that ISIS is controlling large portions of land. It is normal in the way North Korea is normal—a nation that is officially recognized by the world community.

The PLO

Take a deep breath and imagine that scenario for a moment—ISIS becoming a country. It sounds absolutely absurd, doesn't it? As preposterous as that may seem, think about this: What if ISIS were to be given a seat at the United Nations?

For many people, that idea might seem ludicrous, but let us compare the case of Palestine. The Palestinians do not control even a fraction of the territory that ISIS controls. They do not have the military or the equipment that ISIS has. Hamas does not have the budget or the resources of ISIS, yet, today, 193 nations recognize Palestine as a nation, most of them in Africa, Asia, and South America. A quick look at a world map would reveal that the countries with the most freedom do not yet officially recognize Palestine as a country. However, on October 30, 2014, Sweden became the first member of the European Union to officially recognize Palestine.[97] Other nations are sure to follow.

The official recognition of Palestine has been a long-time objective of the Palestine Liberation Organization (PLO), which has achieved that objective through terror. If ISIS were to be recognized as a nation, it would be following the footsteps of other nations that have achieved that objective through violence.

Yasser Arafat, the former chairman of the PLO, was the founder of the Fatah party and is considered to be the father of modern terrorism. Arafat's tactics can be directly linked to the methods employed by ISIS. Arafat is not even Palestinian; he was born in Egypt to an Egyptian family and then joined the Muslim Brotherhood in the 1950s. Remember those guys? Yes, they are linked to the Arab Spring in Egypt and, later, to the fall of Libya and to the flow of weapons into Syria. Arafat is known for his brutal violence, which hinted of both communism and Islam. He believed that people respond better to bullets than to speeches. ISIS most likely agrees.

It was Yasser Arafat who said, "We will not bend or fail until the blood of every last Jew from the youngest child to the oldest elder is spilt to redeem our land!"[98] Does that statement sound similar to the words of ISIS?

Merriam-Webster's 11th Collegiate Dictionary defines *terrorism* as, "The use of violent acts to frighten the people in an area as a way of trying to achieve a political goal." The Federal Bureau of Investigation (FBI) in the United States says that international terrorism "affect[s] the conduct of a government by mass destruction, assassination, or kidnapping."[99]

Yasser Arafat and the PLO fit both of these descriptions. In the 1960s, Arafat and his organization were considered to be terrorists, not just by the United States government, but even by countries in the Middle East. A fact that few people like to talk about is how Arafat and his Palestinian followers attacked innocent Israeli civilians and seized control of the Jordanian infrastructure, which led to a bloody conflict with Jordan's King Hussein. This is known as Black September, during which four Western airliners were hijacked and one was blown up on a runway in Cairo.

Everyone thinks the Jews were the only ones against Arafat, but, in reality, Jordanians no longer welcomed Arafat's pro-Palestinian movement. So, Arafat fled to Lebanon, where he quickly triggered a bloody civil war that Israel would soon have to deal with. The Palestinians were not the problem; the problem was the madman running the pro-Palestinian movement—and he was not even Palestinian!

At the 1972 Summer Olympic in Munich, Germany, the PLO murdered eleven Israeli athletes in cold blood. The Olympic victims' only crime had been being born Jewish. In 1974, the PLO killed twenty-one schoolchildren at Ma'alot. Four years later, they killed thirty-five and wounded eighty-five in an attack on a tourist bus.

Over and over, bombs were set off in civilian areas, innocent children were both targeted and killed, planes were hijacked, bombs were set off at hotels and restaurants, slaughtering bystanders. Over and over, the West vowed to stop the terrorism. But did they? Was the PLO targeted and destroyed, and was Arafat brought to justice?

Quite the opposite. In July 2000, U.S. president Bill Clinton hosted Yasser Arafat and Israeli prime minister Ehud Barak. The Israeli prime minister offered Arafat "a Palestinian state in Gaza and 92 percent of the West Bank, and a capital in East Jerusalem."[100] An offer of that magnitude had never before been put on the table. Arafat rejected the offer and walked away empty-handed. Yasser was a terrorist. He didn't want peace unless it involved the total annihilation of Israel. However, he was awarded the Nobel Peace Prize, and, during his funeral, he was remembered as a selfless statesman. His organization was taken off the lists of international terrorists. Arafat's terrorism worked: it brought appeasement.

The spirit of Arafat lives on in ISIS, which considers the West to be weak and unable to handle long-term conflict. Like Yasser Arafat and the PLO, it intends to inflict the maximum amount of pain and terror possible. ISIS cannot be reasoned with. They do not want 92 percent of the land they seek. They want 100 percent, along with the absolute destruction of their enemies. They will keep coming back until they destroy their enemies and make all people submit to Islam.

Hezbollah

The PLO is not alone. Look at the militant group Hezbollah, which presents another case study of how the world has given in to the demands of terrorism. Hezbollah, also known as "the Party of Allah," is a radical Shia terrorist group that was established to destroy Israel and to fight against Western imperialism.

As a former U.S. Marine, I am deeply saddened by Hezbollah. In 1983, Hezbollah bombed the marine barracks in Beirut, killing 299 French and American service members.[101] The killing of 220 Marines and eighteen sailors that day was the biggest single day of loss of American military personnel since World War II.

Along with its long history of bombing embassies, of kidnapping, and of attacking civilian targets, Hezbollah also kidnapped, tortured, and killed U.S. Marine Corps Colonel William R. Higgins and CIA officer William Buckley in 1991.[102]

The worldwide operation of Hezbollah receives millions of dollars of support every year from Iran; it claims that it is attacking globally because the Jewish influence is everywhere. Hezbollah leader Hassan Nasrallah once stated, "If all the Jews were gathered in Israel, it would save us the trouble of going after them world-wide."[103]

After seeing Hezbollah meet its objectives through terror, the British Foreign Office said, "We have reconsidered our position on no contact with Hezbollah, in light of more positive recent political developments in Lebanon, including the formation of the national unity government in which Hezbollah are participating. We are exploring certain contacts at an official level with Hezbollah's political wing, including MPs."[104]

European peace activists are known to attend Hezbollah conferences on active resistance to Israel, and the UK considers only the "military" wing of Hezbollah to be a terrorist group. "Some Europeans believe that Hezbollah plays a stabilizing role in Lebanon and that to list them [as a terrorist organization] would disrupt the country's stability."[105]

When looking for a solution to the violence in Syria, the United Nations arranged for one of its representatives to meet with Hezbollah to discuss the best way to move forward.[106]

Have things changed since the early attacks from Hezbollah or the PLO? Does it pay less to be a terrorist today than it did before? This does not seem to be the case for Hamas and the Palestinian Authority. Like ISIS, both Hamas and the Palestinian Authority are hell-bent on the destruction of Israel, once again proving that, at some time or another, all roads seem to lead to attacks on Israel.

Hamas

Hamas is an Islamic pro-Palestinian terrorist organization in Palestine. It is an offshoot of the Muslim Brotherhood, as can be seen in Article Two of its 1988 Charter.[107] This charter provides some very interesting reading.

Article Eight is only one sentence long, but it looks like what you might find in an ISIS campaign: "Allah is its [Hamas's] target, the Prophet is its model, the Koran its constitution: Jihad is its path and death for the sake of Allah is the loftiest of its wishes."[108]

In case you feel that, somehow, there might be a slight chance of reaching a peaceful solution with Hamas, read Article Thirteen; it throws the idea of peace out the window.

> [Peace] initiatives, and so-called peaceful solutions and international conferences, are in contradiction to the principles of the Islamic Resistance Movement. Abusing any part of Palestine is abuse directed against part of religion. Nationalism of the Islamic Resistance Movement is part of its religion. Its members have been fed on that. For the sake of hoisting the banner of Allah over their homeland they fight.[109]

Where do you start to negotiate with that view?

Hamas is one of the most ruthless terrorist organizations in the world. It is difficult to measure which organization, Fatah or Hamas, has the most momentum for evil acts against humanity, but Hamas is working hard to obtain the title.

Though Hamas continues to terrorize innocent people in Israel, former U.S. president Jimmy Carter supports it and had demanded that it be fully recognized as representative of the people of Palestine instead of being labeled as a terrorist organization. He believes that Hamas's legitimacy as a political actor must be accepted because Palestine represents a substantial portion of the population. At no time has Carter asked Hamas to lay down its weapons, stop killing children, or refrain from persecuting others.[110]

On November 5, 2014, fourteen people were killed or wounded when a representative from Hamas drove a white van into a crowd of pedestrians in the predominantly Arab neighborhood of Sheik Jarrah.[111]

Before you hear someone blaming Israel for all the current violence due to their occupation of the Palestinian homeland, just remember that Hamas is also banned in Jordan.

Still not convinced that ISIS could one day be fully recognized as a nation? Can you imagine a world in which ISIS could apply for aid from the United Nations? ISIS activities would actually be paid for by the taxpayers of the United States. No need to imagine, because the equivalent is happening every day.

Let us look again at the example of the Palestinian Authority, which presents a similar situation. The Israel Ministry of Foreign Affairs Web site says,

> The Palestinian Authority pays monthly salaries to Palestinian prisoners serving time in Israeli prisons for terrorism-related offences. These salaries are calculated as a function of the number of years spent in prison. This means in effect that the terrorists who carried out the most horrific attacks receive the highest salaries.[112]

The Web site goes on to say,

> The Palestinian Authority is highly dependent on foreign aid. This money, which supports the PA budget, is fungible to meet payments for imprisoned and released terrorists. For example, in 2012 the PA paid over $75 million to terrorists in Israeli prisons and $78 million to the families of deceased terrorists (including suicide bombers). Together, these amounts account for over 16% of the annual foreign donations and grants to the PA budget.[113]

In many ways, peace does not have a chance, because terrorism has higher rewards. CBN News reported,

> "As soon as a terrorist commits an act of terrorism against an innocent civilian in Israel—whether that's cutting the throat of a child or stabbing a man standing at a bus or blowing up a building," [Edwin] Black said. "As soon as that man does that, he goes on a special salary from the Palestinian Authority, under Palestinian law—a law known as the Law of the Prisoner."[114]

Terrorism is also being incentivized by special salaries subsidized by money from the international community. Most likely, the money that is paid to terrorists of the most heinous crimes comes from the 400 million dollars of U.S. aid per year.[115] The more Israelis a terrorist kills, the more time he will serve in prison; thus, he will collect more money during his imprisonment. Apparently, murder can be an excellent career choice that pay well for one's family.

A few years ago, Brother Yun and I were driving in Jerusalem to a meeting with the Knesset, the legislative committee of Israel, to share the Chinese vision of Back to Jerusalem with the Israeli government officials. I saw a sign depicting an American Indian with a feather in his hair. In big letters, the sign read, "Ask me about land for peace." The American Indians gave away land in hopes of establishing peace, but, in the end, had neither. The sign made a very powerful point.

Is Hamas or the Palestinian Authority any better than ISIS? Is either of them any more organized? Actually, it is the other way around. ISIS is more prepared than were Hamas, the PLO, Hezbollah, and the Palestinian Authority; and, from what we have witnessed in the past, it would not seem out of place if ISIS became a recognized country and received international aid.

NINE

ISIS: The World's Conundrum

If ISIS seems like a problem that affects only the Middle East and will never reach the white-picket-fence, cul-de-sac neighborhoods of middle-class Western civilization, then it might come as a surprise that ISIS supporters are worldwide, and its numbers are growing.

Some people believe that radical Islamic groups like ISIS are small and isolated, made up of a few jihadists who hide in desert caves and never make it to the West, or, if they do, are found only in big cities, never in areas that are highly guarded by home security systems and mall police.

Militant Muslims in Europe

Unfortunately, support for ISIS is on the rise in the West, making the terrorist group even more powerful. And its presence is on the rise, as well. Its presence influences its support, and vice versa. In fact, the number of French supporters of ISIS in the millennial age group exceeds the number of millennial supporters of the current French president, François Hollande. Nearly one out of every three or four French citizens between the ages of 18–24 supports ISIS. That means that there is 27 percent support for ISIS and just 18 percent support for President Hollande.[116]

There are now more than twice as many British Muslims fighting for ISIS than there are serving in the British armed forces, according to a British member of Parliament. Furthermore, some Germans are leaving their cushy, Western European lifestyles and going to the front lines to fight alongside other members of the terrorist organization. And after fighting, they may return with their extremism still intact. As of the writing of this book, as many as 150 Islamic fighters have already returned to their homeland and are walking among other German citizens every day.[117]

According to a CNN report, the small, quiet country of Finland tops the list as having the highest percentage of jihadists to leave Europe to fight with ISIS. Tuomas Portaankorva, chief inspector of Finland's intelligence police Supo said,

> There might be some inaccuracies in these numbers because of difficulty in head count but the end result is in the right direction, in other words in terms of Europe we can be counted right up there at the top.[118]

The ISIS black flag is increasingly being used as an icon at protests, such as the one that was openly waved in the streets of the Netherlands on July 21, 2014.[119] A photo of an iPhone displaying the ISIS flag in front of the White House exploded all over Facebook and Twitter, with members of ISIS claiming on social media to have actually posed for the photo on location. Whether it was photoshopped or not, let's not forget that al-Baghdadi already threatened to attack New York City when he was released from prison in Iraq.

ISIS has announced a five-year plan to take back European countries that were once under Islamic control, such as Spain and Portugal.[120]

After watching and reading about the many atrocities committed by ISIS, it would seem impossible to find individuals, let alone groups of people, who support the group, but many parts of Europe are home to Islamic jihadists calling for war.

Europe is dealing with a sudden increase in the Muslim population and a sharp decrease in the number of ethnic Europeans. The birth rates of Muslim immigrant populations have exploded, while the birth rates of European populations have experienced negative growth. Concern over this phenomenon cannot merely be written off as Islamaphobic; the numbers and the hard data of this trend point to a future that will be very much in ISIS's favor.

I stood with a pastor in England on the roof of his newly acquired building, and he asked, "Do you see that church right there?" He pointed to a beautiful stone church across the street that had a majestic steeple that reached to the sky.

"Yes," I said. The massive structure was hard to miss. It was the biggest building on the street and gave off a gloriously warm presence on that rainy, British afternoon.

"That is now a mosque. Muslims are coming into the UK with foreign money, buying old churches, and turning them into mosques. They purchased that particular church because they wanted to have the Islamic crescent hoisted up higher than most other structures in the city."

I almost gasped for air. It was tragic. A beautiful British church was going to be turned into a mosque. It was not just the transformation of the building that caused the shock; it was because it was indicative of what was happening all over Europe.

Muslims are still a minority in Belgium; but, in its capital, Brussels, Islam is already the largest religion. One can find signs that say, "Welcome to Belgistan."

In the UK, there are at least eighty-five Sharia courts that operate independently of the British legal system, and which have the authority to solve local Muslim problems.[121]

Sweden, whose very flag is a symbol of Christianity with its yellow cross on a blue banner, has issued a document listing fifty-five zones in which Swedish police can no longer go. These areas now belong to Muslim criminal gangs that effectively control the areas.[122]

Although Swedish police officers are not allowed to go after Muslim lawbreakers, the "thought police" still go after those who speak up about what is going on. Sweden's newspaper *Expressen* used hackers to get the e-mail addresses and identities of those who have been critical about Islamization through immigration, and who have expressed those thoughts online.

In 2013, the Swedes were shocked to see that the Stockholm suburb Husby was taken over by angry immigrants, mainly Muslim, for a week. Cars were burned and police stations, schools, and businesses were attacked.

Sweden has the most open asylum policies and the most generous social welfare for immigrants in Europe. The country has taken in more than 11,000 refugees from Syria since 2012, which, percentage-wise, is more than any other European country. It also is now home to more than 100,000 Iraqis and 40,000 Somalis. About one-fifth of its population is made up of first- or second generation immigrants, many of whom are Muslim.[123]

Islam in the West

Violence and religious persecution are directly related to the growth of Islam in any given population. In his book *Slavery, Terrorism and Islam: The Historical Roots and Contemporary*

Threat, Dr. Peter Hammond explores what an increasing Muslim population means for countries all over the world.

In nations where the Muslims population is under 2 percent, the minority group is not considered to be a threat to other citizens. This is the current case in the United States, Canada, Norway, and China. However, when the Muslim population is between 2 and 5 percent, the minority begins recruiting from the more oppressed sectors of society, such as prisons, gangs, and so forth. When the population exceeds 5 percent, it begins to exert power and put pressure on local businesses and some sectors of the government for things like dietary restrictions.[124]

As the population increases, Sharia courts start to appear, and violent reactions to non-Islamic code within other sectors of society are experienced. When 60 to 80 percent of the population is Muslim, persecution, jihad, and ethnic cleansing are adopted, with the goal of obtaining a 100 percent Muslim population, ushering in the peace of Dar-es-Salaam, the Islamic House of Peace. This is what we see in Afghanistan, Saudi Arabia, Somalia, and Yemen. However, peace is never really achieved for radical jihadists.[125]

As the number of Muslims increase in Europe, indicators of support for radical jihad Islamic ideology is also increasing.

Consider the following data collected by thereligionofpeace.com:

> ICM Research Poll: 20 percent of British Muslims sympathize with 7/7 bombers [the London suicide bombings of July 7, 2005].
>
> GfK NOP Research: 1 in 4 British Muslims say 7/7 bombings were justified.
>
> Pew Research: 31 percent of Turks support suicide attacks against Westerners in Iraq.

World Public Opinion: 42 percent of Turks approve of some or most groups that attack Americans (45 percent oppose it).

HLN.be: 16 percent of young Muslims in Belgium state terrorism is "acceptable."

Populus Poll (2006): 12 percent of young Muslims in Britain (and 12 percent overall) believe that suicide attacks against civilians in Britain can be justified. In addition, 1 in 4 Muslims support suicide attacks against British troops.

Pew Research (2007): 26 percent of younger Muslims in America believe suicide bombings are justified; 35 percent of young Muslims in Britain believe suicide bombings are justified (24 percent overall); 42 percent of young Muslims in France believe suicide bombings are justified (35 percent overall).

Pew Research (2011): 8 percent of Muslims in America believe suicide bombings are often or sometimes justified (81 percent never).

Federation of Student Islamic Societies: About 1 in 5 Muslim students in Britain (18 percent) would not report a fellow Muslim planning a terror attack.

ICM Research Poll: 25 percent of British Muslims disagree that a Muslim has an obligation to report terrorists to police.

Populus Poll (2006): 16 percent of British Muslims believe suicide attacks against Israelis are justified; 37 percent believe Jews in Britain are a "legitimate target."

Pew Research (2011): 5 percent of American Muslims have a favorable view of al-Qaeda (14 percent can't make up their minds).

Pew Research (2011): 1 in 10 native-born Muslim-Americans have a favorable view of al-Qaeda.

Al-Jazeera (2006): 49.9 percent of Muslims polled support Osama bin Laden.

ICM Research Poll: 40 percent of British Muslims want Sharia in the UK.

GfK NOP Research: 28 percent of British Muslims want Britain to be an Islamic state.

GfK NOP Research: 68 percent of British Muslims support the arrest and prosecution of anyone who insults Islam.

MacDonald Laurier Institute: 62 percent of Muslims want Sharia in Canada (15 percent want to make it mandatory).

BBC Poll: 1 in 10 British Muslims support killing a family member over "dishonor."

The *Middle East Quarterly*: 91 percent of honor killings are committed by Muslims worldwide.

The *National Post*: 95 percent of honor killings in the West are perpetrated by Muslim fathers and brothers or their proxies.

A survey of Muslim women in Paris suburbs found that three-quarters of them wear their masks out of fear, including fear of violence.

Policy Exchange: 1 in 4 Muslims in the UK have never heard of the Holocaust; only 34 percent of British Muslims believe the Holocaust ever happened.

Policy Exchange: 51 percent of British Muslims believe a woman cannot marry a non-Muslim; only 51 percent believe a Muslim woman may marry without a guardian's consent.

Policy Exchange: Up to 52 percent of British Muslims believe a Muslim man is entitled to up to four wives.

Policy Exchange: 61 percent of British Muslims want homosexuality punished.

GfK NOP Research: 62 percent of British Muslims do not believe in the protection of free speech; only 3 percent adopt a "consistently pro-freedom of speech line."

ICM Research Poll: 58 percent of British Muslims believe insulting Islam should result in criminal prosecution.

Pew Research Global (2006): Only 7 percent of British Muslims think of themselves as British first (81 percent say "Muslim" rather than "Briton").

Policy Exchange (2006): 31 percent of Muslims in Britain identify more with Muslims in other countries than with non-Muslim Brits.

Die Welt (2012): 46 percent of Muslims in Germany hope there will eventually be more Muslims than Christians in Germany.

Wenzel Strategies (2012): 12 percent of Muslim-Americans believe blaspheming Islam should be punishable by death; 43 percent of Muslim-Americans believe people of other faiths have no right to evangelize Muslims; 32 percent of Muslims in America believe that Sharia should be the supreme law of the land.[126]

Even a cursory look at these numbers should be a concern to all. As horrible as ISIS is, the rise of support for the terrorist organization from Europe is a powerful indicator of what may come. The United Nations has been seeking to create an anti-blasphemy law, which would make any anti-Islamic statement an international crime. Large groups in the EU also support this measure.

A very clear strategy is being implemented by many Muslim immigrants: first begging for acceptance and then demanding conformity.

Muslim immigrants go to Europe and America for freedom from persecution and for economic opportunities to provide for their families. Many may start out with mainly personal motives. "We cannot stay here any longer," one Iraqi woman said to me in November 2014. She was living in a schoolhouse after having escaped from ISIS. "We just want to go to Europe."

She pleaded with me as if I had the power to grant her a visa.

"We can't live here like this. We have no food, no heat, no money. We just want to go to Europe." She stood with others who were living at the school together with her. All of them had barely escaped ISIS. She put her hands up in the air as she spoke of the desperate situation. "Our babies do not have milk. We have no way to cook our food. The rain comes in through the roof of this schoolhouse."

Life in Iraq was the only life that this woman had ever known. She had never been out of Iraq, let alone to Europe, yet she was positive that all her problems would be solved if she were allowed to travel to Europe.

Many Muslims travel to Europe, make homes, and beg for the equal rights and equal treatment that the rest of the population has. However, it seems that, somewhere along the way, the Muslim immigrant population stops begging for acceptance and begins to demand conformity from the host country. It insists that the host country adapt its rules and its lifestyle. Many Muslims insist on both an acceptance and an enforcement of Islamic law.

It seems as if immigrant Muslim communities believe that the lack of Islam in their host country is the sole cause of all the problems.

Rashid Hmami is a former Muslim from Morocco who converted to Christianity. He hosts a popular television program where viewers can call in and have their questions answered.

A Swedish ISIS supporter named Sheikh Ahmed called in and did not waste any time in declaring jihad on the Swedes. "We will fight wherever we find you. Even in Sweden, until you say that there is no God but Allah."

"You say that you will fight everyone till they become Muslims?"

"Until the last day of our lives we will fight against Sweden and all of Europe." He talked in a very calm manner. He did not sound excited or emotional. His message was clear.

"And you live in Sweden?" asked Rashid.

"I am in Sweden," he replied.

"And from the infidels, you get their social benefits?" inquired Rashid.

"No, we get our allowance from God only."

"You exploit and take money from the state," Rashid pointed out.

"No, it is not their money. It comes from Allah."

"So, why not enjoy the money in your own country? Why are you living among the infidels?"

"We are living here, and it is our plight to spread our religion," he responded.

Rashid knows the Islamic teaching and replied, "But you know very well that it is haram [sin] to live in an infidel country like that."

"An Islamic country is Allah's country, which encompasses the whole world."[127]

Ahmed went on to say that infidels must be killed and that mercy would be shown only if they paid *jizya*. He believed Sweden owed him financial social assistance because (1) he was a Muslim, and (2) the Swedes were infidels; he also believed that the justification for ISIS killing the Iraqi Christians was that they did not pay *jizya*.

Ahmed was not living in Pakistan or Yemen, where his words could be overlooked or ignored. He was a Muslim immigrant living in liberal, free, wealthy Sweden, and collecting a pension that he felt he was entitled to.

ISIS in America: Coming to a City Near You

America is not as far along in the Islamization process as Europe is, but ISIS is actively trying to recruit Islamic jihadists there and is proving successful.

In early September 2014, Alton Alexander Nolen was only thirty years old and fresh out of jail (with a history of drug possession and distribution, as well as assault on police officers). He was also newly employed at the Vaughan Foods processing plant in Moore, Oklahoma, on the outskirts of Oklahoma City.

He had converted to Islam in 2013, and most of the people who were friends with him on Facebook knew him by his Muslim name, Jah'Keem Yisrael. Prior to his conversion, he had not posted anything about religion. But afterward, Nolen had become engaged in international politics and had begun posting anti-American pictures of Osama bin Laden and the 9/11 attacks on the World Trade Center, blaming the attacks on America's involvement in the Middle East. He had also posted pictures of Islamic beheadings, which had started to intrigue him. In March 2014, he posted a picture of a partially severed head with a caption that read, "This do we find the clear precedent that explains the particular penchant of Islamic terrorists to behead their victims, it is merely another precedent bestowed upon by their Prophet."[128]

Nolen was a six-foot-tall African American who wore a "tight fade" haircut and was growing out his beard. He could be found reading his Koran and wearing typical Middle Eastern-inspired clothing and a white prayer cap.

His new Muslim outlook was a far cry from the rapper lifestyle he had aspired to when he was younger. Before he became Muslim, he liked to wear baggy, stonewashed jeans that hung down past the top of his thigh, fully exposing his underwear. He'd spent his younger days working out in the gym and taking "selfies" to share with others.

Now, he posted pictures of himself holding up his index finger, which is a common gesture among Muslims symbolizing that there is only one god, who is Allah. It is also the common sign of ISIS in social media pictures.

Retired mechanic Fred Fletcher lived directly below Nolen's $450/month apartment, and he remembered that Nolen had been an extremely quiet tenant. "I tried to be friendly and said hi on at least three occasions, he didn't even turn his head, he looked straight through me," Fred recalled. "He moved in less than a year ago, but you never heard much from him, he went to work in his SUV and came home, he never had any visitors, he was a loner."[129] In fact, Nolen had refused to let the maintenance man into his apartment when something needed to be fixed, because Nolen was a Muslim and didn't want non-Muslims in his house.[130] Those who finally obtained access into Nolen's apartment found that everything was neat, clean, and tidy.

When Nolen was fired from his job in September 25, 2014, he immediately drove home, grabbed a knife, and placed it in his shoe. The knife belonged to the company, and he had used it to cut vegetables, boxes, and so forth. He was going to show the infidels what he thought of them.

Although Nolen had praised beheadings on his Facebook page, this time, he was the one who would do the beheading. He had three specific people in mind. One of them was his forty-three-year-old white coworker, Traci Johnson, who had found herself in an argument with Nolen about race.

On that day, Nolen left his home at the Colonial Apartments, a common residence for single males working at Vaughan Foods, and jumped into his maroon 1999 GMC SUV with one destination in mind—his former workplace.

Just after 4:00 p.m., Nolen arrived at the front of the processing plant and struck a vehicle before turning off the engine of his SUV. He didn't pull into a parking space; he just left his car right where he had stopped it.

Nolen walked inside and saw fifty-four-year-old Colleen Hufford in the front office. Born in Germany and raised in Montana, she was an Oklahoma transplant. Hufford was a stout lady but was no challenge for thirty-year-old Nolen. Hufford was not Nolen's initial target but was nevertheless attacked.

Nolen stabbed Hufford several times in the back of the neck. The stab wounds were most likely enough to kill her, but Nolen needed something more. He needed to kill the infidel in the same manner that Muhammad had killed infidels. He reached around and sawed back and forth, severing her head while shouting Koranic verses.

Nolen did not have a sword. He had only a produce knife that had been used for cutting vegetables and fruits. When other coworkers saw what was happening, they began to fight Nolen by kicking him and throwing chairs at him. Then, when Nolen got a chance to stab Traci Johnson, one of his original targets, he took it.

At 4:15, someone called 911 to report the stabbing. During the call, Traci was being stabbed, but then shots rang out, ending the attack.

Mark Vaughan, company CEO and reserve county deputy, had shot Nolen with a rifle that he kept at work. Nolen was seriously wounded but survived the shooting.

Prior to Nolen's attack, there had been speculation that the videos used by ISIS would inspire lone-wolf violence. Nolen's Facebook page contained a photo of Abu Suleiman al-Otaibi, an Iraqi Shia official. The photo had been provided by al-Furqan Media, which had aired the beheading videos.[131]

A Muslim who attends the same mosque as Nolen says that the mosque preaches violence and supports extremist groups like Hamas. It also teaches that all non-Muslims will one day have to make the decision to either covert or live under the caliphate of ISIS. "I was told by two mosque members that if Osama Bin Laden came to their door they would invite him in and would protect him from law enforcement because he's a Muslim brother and we have to protect him from the unbelievers."[132]

Though this gruesome attack has been politically expedited into the category of "workplace violence," clearly it was motivated by Islam and possibly by ISIS. Nolen's tipping point might have been work-related, but he was Muslim and inspired by Islam, even shouting Koranic teachings during the murder.

The following day, not even thirty miles from Vaughan Foods, Jacob Mugambi Muriithi, a Kenyan Muslim who claims to represent ISIS, threatened to cut off someone else's head.

ISIS has been inspiring many young Muslims around the world. No place is exempt. Both of the above events took place in Oklahoma, one of the most conservative, Christian states, and incidentally the only state in which every single county voted against President Obama's reelection in 2012. If ISIS-inspired attacks can take place in Oklahoma, they can take place anywhere. In the next chapter, we will look at how ISIS excels in recruiting such a diverse group of followers.

TEN

Recruits and Military Equipment

ISIS has one of the most sophisticated media operations ever employed by an Islamic terrorist group, and much of it is dedicated to recruitment purposes. ISIS has recruited supporters from all over the world, and it has a keen eye on the United States, looking for opportunities to recruit Americans from every walk of life.

You might think that members of ISIS are sitting in Iraq or Syria at their computers trying to convince Americans to board a plane and come join them. This is not the case. *Americans* recruit Americans to join ISIS.

> "Westerners are involved, especially in the recruitment and social media dissemination of the whole ISIS brand," Mubin Shaikh, a former Taliban recruiter who operated from his hometown of Toronto before becoming a national security operative in Canada, told *International Business Times*. "Look at the videos they're making. You think those people were trained in Syria and Iraq? Those people were trained in the West."[133]

When ISIS recruiters are in America, what are they looking for? How do they identify someone who might possibly be the next Alton Nolen?

According to Shaikh, there are specific things that recruiters for ISIS are looking for, including...

- People who are new to Islam.
- People who are having problems at home, making them vulnerable.
- People who have no prior connection to Syria or Iraq.
- People who are extremely ignorant about religion.

> "People collaborating with IS can be ordinary people," said Aymenn Jawad al-Tamimi, a Shillman-Ginsburg Fellow at the Middle East Forum. "They don't have to be religious fanatics. They could be anyone provided you give your pledge of allegiance to ISIS."[134]

Much of the recruiting in America is taking place in prisons, where Islam gives a sense of hope to the hopeless and renewed purpose to those who feel downtrodden and neglected by society. Islam gives a reason and a purpose for the injustice of the past but creates a victim-like mentality in its followers. This effect is the complete opposite of a coming-to-Jesus moment, which leads to freedom and forgiveness.

Recruitment in the prison systems focuses on African-American men and Hispanics, with whom the race card is heavily used. Felons are being told that Christianity is the religion that has enslaved them and that Islam is the African/Hispanic religion that will restore them to their rightful place.

ISIS recruiters have been using the racial tensions of Ferguson, Missouri, to find new recruits. After a white cop shot and killed an unarmed young black male who was trying to attack him, ISIS recruiters started using social media to reach out to potential members.

"[I] thought u guys back in Ferguson were supposed to be Free & that u had equal rights," read one tweet from an ISIS recruiter. "I'd really like to know what changed? Justice and Equality is under the Shari'ah Law. You'll never get it under Democracy."[135]

Universities, colleges, and churches are also places where ISIS recruits people for their purposes. According to an imam in Canada who has received multiple death threats, imams who teach against ISIS in mosques become targets.[136]

The U.S.-led bombing campaign targeting ISIS has not slowed down recruiting at all. In fact, since the bombing campaign started in the fall of 2014, the number of recruits from the West has increased.[137]

According to the Clarion Project, which researches ISIS recruiting methods, ISIS members are even looking for recruits among lonely young girls and single mothers in America. They are going in to chat rooms on the Internet and meeting young women who are desperate for love and acceptance. Muslim men are recruiting these young women who are looking for Mr. Tall, Mr. Dark, and Mr. Handsome. Militants offer them a home, a man, love, and protection. They tell them that they will be the mother of a household, cooking and taking care of a loving home as Allah has intended. At a time of financial difficulty in America, the offer seems very promising to many young and lonely females.

Not all ISIS supporters are lonely single females or incarcerated in prison systems. One business owner in upstate New York was arrested in September 2014 for recruiting people to go and fight for ISIS and for plotting to kill Americans on American soil.[138]

ISIS is active in the United States, and it is safe to say that, among other things, it is also the most successful terrorist recruiter in the history of the world. The Islamic caliphate that it dreams of is global, requiring our immediate attention.

ISIS's success in the Middle East is attracting young men and women from the around the world to join its cause. ISIS always has a need for recruits to come and join in the fight in Iraq and Syria, but it also needs help in the fight on American and European soil, and there seem to be many willing participants.

"If you want to recruit young men into the Marine Corps," staff sergeant Lance Healey told me one day after his return from deployment in the Persian Gulf, "you have to go big, you have to show them the big picture. You have to prove to them that you are the most elite and you are the best. That is the best tool for recruitment."

Staff sergeant Healey was formerly a recruiter for the United States Marine Corps and was in charge of Third Battalion, First Marines STA platoon, or the Surveillance and Target Acquisition platoon, better known as the scout snipers.

As a recruiter, Healey had to know how to get into the psyche of the young American male. If ISIS wanted to recruit Americans to leave their life in America to fight in the desert sands of the Middle East, it would have to use similar tactics.

As a former Marine, I have learned the bare bones of assessing a military threat. I do not claim to be an expert in the field, but I have had both experience in and exposure to interpreting the damage that a military unit can pose.

When I examine the growing military capability of ISIS, I am convinced that its military capacity is on par with many military threats that can inflict damage on our interests on a global scale. Experience on the battlefield is on the side of ISIS, but administrative experience of large-scale mechanized attacks is not at the moment in their favor. However, this is slowly changing.

The fact that ISIS is the most powerful and most funded terrorist organization ever to exist is a great recruitment advantage, and it would have been one of the main things that staff sergeant Healey would have emphasized if he were recruiting for them. ISIS is recruiting young American men and women who feel detached from others and have a need to belong and to be respected. ISIS sells them a bill of goods guaranteeing that people will respect them. To ISIS, fear equals respect, and it has all the tools to inflict the maximum amount of fear.

As we have seen, ISIS is basically its own country. That is more and more becoming a reality. Each day that it remains in power is a day in which it becomes stronger as a nation, or, as they like call it, a caliphate.

ISIS has already implemented laws, borders, trading mechanisms, and transportation systems, and has provided public services, such as education, to its citizens. It also has a commodity that the rest of the world needs and cannot live without—oil. It already sells oil on a regular basis. It uses the tactic of fear that the international community would rather appease than confront, since past scenarios have taught us that appeasement is the international community's pillar tenet of conflict resolution.

ISIS has a standing army that is better equipped than other militaries in the region. Not even the American military has been able to stop its advancements. Even though bombing raids have been launched against it, ISIS has defied the odds and continues to gain ground.

Most countries shake in fear at an American attack, but ISIS has not flinched. This is largely due to its recruiting of young Americans. Who else can defy the American military and win?

The Iraqi Army has been trained and equipped by the American and NATO forces, but ISIS has sliced straight through their lines of defense like a knife through warm butter.

ISIS Armed with Special Training and Military Equipment

The Upper Hand in Special Training

International recruits are essential to ISIS's establishment of a global Islamic caliphate, but they are not the only weapons of warfare. ISIS members have also received special training and have procured specialized military equipment from one of the most unlikely sources.

It seems that these tools in the hands of poorly trained terrorists would not be such a big deal, but it would be a grave mistake to assume that ISIS soldiers are not well-trained; it seems that the United States not only supplied arms to ISIS but provided troop training, as well. Remember those "moderate" rebels whom the Western powers were so eager to support against the cruel government of Syria? Well, according to Jordanian officials, the moderate rebels were secretly trained by U.S. soldiers at a base in Jordan in 2012, and were equipped with battlefield knowledge by specialized instructors.[140] U.S., Jordan, and Turkey all assisted in a coordinated effort to provide training for the moderate rebels in Safawi, Jordan. Many of these trained troops eventually joined ISIS.

These militants are now some of the top echelon warriors training future fighters. Not only are they training the jihadists of today, but they are thinking ahead and training the fighters of tomorrow.

As mentioned earlier, in villages now occupied by ISIS, young boys have been taken from their families to be trained as jihadists.

They are swearing their allegiance to Islam and ISIS in a fashion that is very similar to the children and teenagers in the Hitler youth program or the young pioneers of Mao Zedong.

They are indoctrinated with the Koran. Videos are being shown in Iraq of little boys as young as six years old standing up against a wall and reading the Koran over and over. These young, impressionable boys are made to witness public beheadings. Their immature minds are inundated with every gruesome detail of a decapitation. When ISIS fighters are injured in battle, the young boys automatically become blood donors, and every one of them is trained to become a suicide bomber.[140] One of these children could easily be used as a walking low-tech biological warfare machine.

The Upper Hand in Military Equipment

As talked about earlier, ISIS was equipped by Libya in Syria. ISIS used the equipment and experience from Syria to fight in Iraq. Then it captured the weapon caches of the 2nd and 3rd Iraqi Army divisions when it attacked Mosul, equipping them to capture caches from the 4th and 12th Iraqi Army divisions in Salah al Din and around Kirkuk, and another division in Diyala.[141]

In addition to the supplies that it was able to get from Libya, Syria, and Iraq, ISIS has also been extremely fortunate to acquire additional supplies from a U.S. airdrop originally intended for the Kurds. According to ISIS, the United States air-dropped twenty-eight bundles of equipment, including medical supplies, weapons, and ammunition.[142]

In addition, in 2013, the U.S. military misplaced more than $420 million worth of military equipment in Afghanistan, which contained 156,000 pieces of military hardware, including sophisticated weapons systems and vehicle and communications gear.

No matter how you slice it, the most brutal terrorist organization in world history is being indirectly supplied with military goods from the most advanced military in the world. This is just plain bad news.

A quick inventory would show that ISIS currently has fifty-two 155-mm M198 howitzers, the king of the battlefield. These howitzers have a range of twenty miles and can incorporate GPS targeting systems. Furthermore, ISIS has thirty T-55 tanks and as many as ten T-72 tanks, both of which are heavily armored and provide an awesome amount of firepower for ground invasions. The T-72 is also fitted with a 125-mm gun and antiaircraft weapon system.[143]

In addition, ISIS has the M1 Abram tank, which is sixty-eight tons of raw, battle-craving steel. This massive beast is an oldie but goodie and is unmatched on the battlefield.

I remember driving through the northern desert sands of Kuwait in the 1990s, observing the graveyard of T-72s and T-52s that were used by Saddam's Iraqi Republican Guard in the First Gulf War. Tanks littered the empty desert, which was a gold mine for a young infantrymen like me. I scavenged through the area and pulled out small military treasures that I took back to the States with me. Not one damaged American Abram could be found. The battle had been a one-sided bloodbath. The Abrams had easily trounced on and destroyed every tank in sight, and then had driven away virtually unscathed.

ISIS now has the same tank. It also has at least 1,500 armored Humvees; RPG-7 rocket launchers; Scud missiles; AIM-9 Sidewinder air-to-air missiles; IED-resistant MRAP transport vehicles; and FIM-92 Stingers. In addition, it has enough flak jackets, Kevlar helmets, M-16s, and ammunition to provide three sets to every soldier fighting for ISIS. That is more than U.S. soldiers sometimes have.

As representative Tom McClintock of California said in a speech on the House floor, "The Islamic State is armed to the teeth—with American equipment."[144]

There are rumors that ISIS has even obtained helicopters and jet fighters—Russian-made MiG jets. They have also captured pilots from both Syria and Iraq to train ISIS jihadists.[145]

American jet pilots are praying that these rumors are true, because they are having a hard enough time identifying targets on the ground without ground troops; but anything in the air is free game for them. An ISIS air force would be an absolute turkey shoot.

Admittedly, ISIS cannot really do much with its airpower against other, better-trained militaries, but it can present some serious danger on the ground in Iraq if unchecked. The advanced technology it currently has, aside from its air capabilities, can do a lot of damage to foreign militaries both on the ground and in the air.

Even more troublesome is that in June 2014, ISIS captured a former chemical weapons facility in Iraq, increasing the possibility that a chemical weapon could be used against local troops in the future.

According to Captain Al Shimkus, Ret., professor of National Security Affairs at the U.S. Naval War College, ISIS may already be thinking of using Ebola as an attack weapon. He said, "The individual exposed to the Ebola Virus would be the carrier. In the context of terrorist activity, it doesn't take much sophistication to go to the next step to use a human being as a carrier."[146]

A terrorist could be purposefully infected with Ebola, then sent out to roam the streets and visit busy theme parks, ball games, movie theaters, shopping malls, and so forth, to infect as many people as possible. The danger is magnified because of the effective recruiting that ISIS has conducted. Now they have nationals who currently possess passports from many different countries, which allow them automatic reentry into their homelands. Low-tech biological warfare is a security risk that must be taken into account when assessing the global threat of ISIS.

It would even be possible for an ISIS operative to infect himself with the sole purpose of infecting as many people as possible, and then eventually get treated for the illness and survive, allowing him to reinfect himself and go back at it again. Self-infecting and early treatment, even if unsuccessful, would also cost valuable resources and deplete scarce medical treatments that could otherwise be used on true victims.

No idea should be left outside of the realm of possibilities with ISIS.

It is assumed that ISIS already has access to eighty-eight pounds of uranium that it obtained from the University of Mosul when it took over the city.[147] And it is searching for more materials to make a bomb. During a raid in March 2014, a document for obtaining nuclear capabilities was found at an ISIS commander's home. It was allegedly written by Abdullah Ahmed al-Meshedani, one of ISIS's senior leaders, and is thought to be authentic. One of the suggestions was for ISIS to offer the Russians access to the Iraqi gas and oil fields in return for nuclear support.[148]

The chances of Russia pulling its current support of Iran and Syria in favor of ISIS seem to be slim at this point, but it is possible. With the money that ISIS currently has, as well as its steady stream of income, its control of resources, and its massive military weapons caches, it would not be impossible for the group to find nuclear capabilities from places like North Korea and the former Soviet Union. The underground black market for nuclear capabilities might be able to put some very creative things together for the right price.

World community leaders, of course, can make a big show of how they would never let that happen, but it is still possible for ISIS to obtain nuclear weapons in the face of incredible odds. After all, for years, Western countries have boasted that they would never ever allow North Korea or Iran to become nuclear powers. How has that worked out?

ISIS has made known its intention to destroy Israel and establish its caliphate in Jerusalem. In 2008, al-Baghdadi proposed to use Iraq as a launching pad for missile attacks against Israel.

These kinds of threats are nothing new to jihadists; anyone who has studied the works of al-Qaeda would be used to hearing these messages. What makes ISIS different is that it has proven that it has the leadership, the willpower, and the means to carry out its threats. It has the financing and the military power. ISIS is currently building up its war chest and training its soldiers to make more gains in the future. If it is unbothered for a few years, it will solidify its position in Iraq and Syria and adjust its focus for later attacks. Israel will be one of its first targets once it is more stable, and the threat of a nuclear war could be a very real danger.

The ISIS Slave Market

The magnitude of the ISIS problem culminates in its attacks on women and children. As mentioned previously, many ISIS fighters "own" sex slaves and/or enter into forced marriages with girls as reward for their service. One ISIS slave market price list included these statements:

> In the name of Allah, most gracious and merciful. We have received news that the demand in women and cattle markets has sharply decreased and that will affected Islamic State revenues as well as the funding of the Mujaheddin

in the battlefield. We have made some changes. Below are the prices of Yazidi and Christian women.[149]

To make sure that every ISIS member received his own slave, ISIS limited the number of sex slaves to three per buyer at one time, unless the buyer was from Turkey, Syria, or the Gulf.[150]

Yazidi girls are popular in the ISIS slave market because many of them have light-colored hair and skin. Some of them also have green or blue eyes, which is very uncommon in the Middle East.

I spent time walking through refugee camps that were full of Yazidi people. I met with families who were fortunate enough to have escaped with their wives and daughters, and I met with families who were not so fortunate. Sex is a taboo subject in the Yazidi culture. Many women would rather die than return to their families with stories of being raped.

Many of the families I have spent time with had stories of other families who had suffered the indignity of rape, but none of the ones I talked with wanted to discuss firsthand experiences. I visited the refugee camps soon after the ISIS invasion, so I understood that the feelings were still raw. Our efforts were to provide aid to them, not wound them further.

The stories of ISIS raping Yazidi and Christian women are heartbreaking enough, but a closer look will reveal something even more disturbing.

It is not only the men of ISIS who are involved in the sex slave industry; the efforts are supported by jihadi women, as well. Female jihadists working with ISIS are forcing women to work as sex slaves. The money from the sales is used to support the war effort. Even more sinister is the fact that the some of the women running the sex rings are from Britain![151]

The sex slaves are kept in brothels that are run by a female police force called the al-Khanssaa Brigade. Thousands of Iraqi women have been forced to work in such brothels, and as many as 3,000 of them are Yazidis. ISIS is giving the British women roles with lots of authority because they have proven to be some of its most loyal followers.

One of the leading women in charge is twenty-year-old Aqsa Mahmood from Glasgow. Several French women are believed to be involved in the brigade, as well. Women who have grown up in European society are aiding the rampage across Syria and Iraq, enslaving Christian and Yazidi girls.

This has become such a huge problem that the United Nations has issued a statement on the barbaric acts of sexual violence that have been perpetrated on young women and children. Nickolay Mladenov and Zainab Hawa Bangura, special representatives of the United Nations, said,

> We condemn, in the strongest terms, the explicit targeting of women and children and the barbaric acts the "Islamic State of Iraq and the Levant" has perpetrated on minorities in areas under its control, and we remind all armed groups that acts of sexual violence are grave human rights violations that can be considered as war crimes and crimes against humanity.[152]

Victims of rape include Iraqi Yazidi, Christian, Turkomen, and Shabak women, as well as teenage boys and girls.

Iraqi News published an article with the following price list for women to be sold as sex slaves.

- A (Yazidi or Christian) woman, aged 40 to 50 years, is for 50,000 dinars [$43 USD].
- The rate of a (Yazidi or Christian) woman, aged 30 to 40 years, is 75,000 dinars [$64 USD].
- The rate for a (Yazidi or Christian) woman, aged 20 to 30 years, is 100,000 dinars [$86 USD].

- A (Yazidi or Christian) girl, aged 10 to 20 years, is for 150,000 dinars [$129 USD].
- A (Yazidi or Christian) child's price, aged 1 to 9 years, is 200,000 dinars [$172 USD].[153]

That last point is staggering. Innocent little girls between the ages of *one and nine* are being subjected to some of the vilest actions on earth, which are being supported and arranged by women who currently carry European passports. These reports really show how desperate the situation is.

Parts of Europe are already getting a small taste of what is being inflicted on Syria and Iraq by ISIS. In the Swedish capital of Stockholm alone, over 700 women and 300 children were raped by Muslim immigrants between January and July of 2013. The number of adolescent young girls who are being raped continues to rise in this quiet Scandinavian country.[154] Sweden, with its growing Muslim population, has become the rape capital of Europe, with sixty-three reported rapes for every 100,000 people. That gives Sweden the second highest number of rapes out of all other countries in the world. According to research, more than 77 percent of these rapes are by Muslim immigrants.[155]

Judeo-Christian ethics in Western countries uphold the value of life and the dignity of every person, including women and children. To imagine these crimes against women and children taking place in the Middle East is difficult enough. To imagine them in a traditional Christian country is sobering, if not shocking. The number of rapes that occur in places like Stockholm, and the violent manner in which they are carried out, might suggest that some of them are not mere acts of individual criminals but have a more sinister resemblance to warfare. It is the same kind of abusive byproduct of warfare that is seen on the battlefield with ISIS.

ISIS feels an Islamic entitlement to the spoils of war, which essentially means that ISIS militants believe they are entitled to the young girls whom they are taking into slavery. ISIS has conquered the Yazidi and Christian areas of Syria and Iraq, and its members feel it is their right to take the booty. This is not just a part of the victor's bounty; it is the code of conduct exhibited by Muhammad himself.

Not all Muslims support this behavior, and it would be wrong to assume that they do; but both the Koran and the prophet Muhammad have set examples that extremist Muslims use as their basic model. The theologically justified crime of owning female slaves is an attack on humanity.

True evil is most prominent in the infliction of pain on the most defenseless people in society. ISIS's attacks on women and children must be stopped at all costs. But we cannot stop them by attacking merely the symptoms; we must not remain passive to the root of the problem.

Christians have the answer, and there has never been a more important time in history to respond to the call of duty. As you read this book, thousands of women and children are being victimized. What can be done? What tools do Christians have at their disposal? We will now take a look at Back to Jerusalem and what it is doing to fight this evil.

ELEVEN

BTJ's Three-Phase Plan

Both Iraq and Syria are home to groups of people who have never heard the message of Jesus Christ. ISIS is storming through the poorest and most spiritually desolate places in the world. This area is part of the "10/40 Window," a term that is very familiar to missionary communities. It was coined by Christian missionary Luis Bush to refer to the countries and people groups located between 10 degrees and 40 degrees north of the equator. Countries like Iraq and Syria that are in this window have the highest levels of poverty, the lowest levels of medical care, the lowest levels of quality of life, and the least access to the gospel.

"The Land Between the Walls"

The 10/40 Window falls mainly between the world's two major walls—the Great Wall of China and the Western Wall of Jerusalem. At Back to Jerusalem, we call this area "the land between the walls." Though this phrase is applied loosely, Chinese missionaries use it interchangeably with the term 10/40 Window.

Like most of the nations in this region, Iraq and Syria have been home to some of the greatest ancient societies—such as the

Sumerian, Akkadian, Assyrian, and Babylonian Empires—but have been strangled by the choking power of Islam. The current struggles in Syria and Iraq have not always been the norm. Both countries used to be a tapestry of religious and ethnic diversity, but with the dawn of Islam, enforced religious homogeny has triumphed.

Except for the Armenian and Syrian minorities, which are ethnically Christian, all the other people groups in Iraq have not yet been reached with the gospel. Large groups of people do not have any known missionaries in their regions. Shia Arabs in the southern part of Iraq, Yazidis, Marsh Arabs, Najdi Bedouins, Surchi, Guarani, Bejalani, Hawrami, northern Kurds, and Luri are largely unreached people groups. Some of these groups are 100 percent unreached, meaning that there is not even one person within them who is known to have been exposed to the message of Jesus Christ.

These people groups are insulated from the gospel because their governments not only disapprove of evangelism within their borders, but they also disapprove of Christian activities in neighboring countries. It is this type of fierce opposition that has led to the formation of radical groups like ISIS. Not only are these governments determined to destroy Christianity in their own countries, but they are equally committed to keeping it from taking hold in surrounding regions.

Why does any of this matter? Why not let non-Christians live as non-Christians?

The land between the walls is at the very heart of the problem with ISIS in Syria and Iraq. Modern Western society has somehow adopted a policy of live and let live, believing that the best policy is to allow societies to fend for themselves, as long as they do not bother anyone else.

Yet Matthew 28:19–20 and Acts 1:8 do not allow Christians the luxury of being inactive in light of the spiritual needs of others.

They *command* Christians to go out and share the good news. Nowhere are Christians commanded to force others to believe. God has always given people a choice. Our mandate is not to convert others but to share the gospel. Sharing is not just expected of Christians; it is our social duty.

The cold, hard truth is that evil, left to fester, both persecutes and grows. Like a cancer, it does not stay isolated and localized; it spreads and infects. Evil conquers and controls. It imposes and kills. It rapes and destroys.

The land between the walls did not ask for Islam; the religion was forced upon it. Iraq and Syria did not ask for Islam; it was forced upon them.

It is the responsibility of the followers of Jesus Christ to take the hope and the light of Truth to the people who live in this land. It is only through the love of Jesus Christ that societies can be transformed and evil can be stopped. Yet, even though Christians have this responsibility, most Christians of the twenty-first century are not responding to the call.

There are currently 7 billion people in the world. Two-thirds of them live in the land between the walls. North and South Americans, South Africans, Australians, and so forth, make up only one-third of the world's population.

Out of the 7 billion people in the world, it is estimated that only 2.18 billion are Christians.[156] According to the Pew Research Center, one hundred years ago, the majority of Christians lived in Europe. That is no longer the case. Now, only a little over one fourth of Christians live in Europe.

The Gospel of Hope

Why is ISIS able to inflict destruction in such an unstoppable manner? Four words: people's lack of hope. If people have never heard the message of the gospel, how are they supposed to resist the enemy? Without Jesus, what is there really to hope for? Overwhelming evil can instill a paralyzing fear and sense of hopelessness.

Since nine out of ten people on the planet who have never heard the gospel message live in the land between the walls, this means that most of the world is living without hope. Yet few Christians—who have the answer to the problem with ISIS—are going to these hopeless areas to share the truth. To put things into perspective, follow the money; you will find that only 0.1 percent of mission funding is being used to share the gospel in the thirty-eight most unevangelized countries.[157] Not even 1 percent of mission funding is going to the neediest areas. In America in 2013, more money was spent on dog food than on spreading the gospel to unreached people groups. To add insult to injury, often, more money is spent on Halloween costumes for pets in America than on mission work in Iraq and Syria.

This is an "ecclesiastical crime" and leaves the lost sheep of the world out in the open as the sacrificial prey of roaming wolves like ISIS. Out of the 594 billion dollars given to churches in 2013 (that is billion with a *b*), a little over 6 percent of it is squandered, and a total of 8 billion dollars is lost due to mismanagement. The amount of money that is actually used to introduce the good news to unreached people is an estimated 32 billion dollars.[158]

The majority of Christian funding, 97 percent of it, does not target non-Christians but rather the very Christians who donate it. It is a type of reinvestment scheme that gives hope to those who already have hope, but ensures that the helpless will remain completely hopeless.

The Three-Phase Plan

Chinese Back to Jerusalem missionaries cannot wait any longer for the Western church to mobilize for the Great Commission, as commanded in Matthew 28:19–20 and Acts 1:8. New Chinese believers who are still being tried by fire in Communist China have been commanded to reach the unreached peoples of the world, and they are doing it in a remarkable way.

The Chinese are training in several different camps around Asia to take the gospel message to the unreached people groups in Iraq. In fact, they have already started to do so. Currently, Chinese Back to Jerusalem missionaries are carrying out a three-phase plan to meet the challenges presented by ISIS.

The three phases are…

1. To provide emergency aid to the Iraqis who have escaped death and are living in refugee camps.
2. To provide missionaries and gospel materials to the refugees living in the camps.
3. To target ISIS with the good news of Jesus Christ, primarily by supplying the Gospel Cloud unit.

Phase One: Providing Emergency Aid

Phase one of the BTJ plan to meet the challenges of ISIS involves providing emergency aid items to the people of Iraq. Back to Jerusalem missionaries have provided such aid to people in the past after several natural disasters (earthquakes, tsunamis, floods, and so forth), but this is the first man-made humanitarian disaster that BTJ has ever officially dealt with. Emergency aid is desperately needed in the refugee camps of Iraq and Syria.

Most families that fled from ISIS in June, July, August, and September of 2014 did not take anything with them but the clothes on their backs. The dire situation required the immediate provision of food, clothing, water, and shelter. Back to Jerusalem was able to provide food, clothes, pots, pans, tents, and yogurt for immediate relief.

Back to Jerusalem is also providing a long-term solution to the problem by setting up small unit Aquaponics for individual refugee families. Aquaponics is a form of farming that BTJ missionaries have adopted and shared with the most rural and the most urban areas of the world alike. Aquaponics was brought to China for BTJ by Travis Hughey, who is an expert in organic farming.

Aquaponics is a sustainable food source that uses fish waste to feed and fertilize vegetables. Aquaponics does not require soil, so it can be used in the most unforgiving land on earth. Instead of soil, the vegetables are planted in rock beds. The water flows through the rock beds to provide nutrients to the plants, and the rock beds provide a natural filtration system that cleans the water flowing back to the fish.

Back to Jerusalem missionaries have used this device all over the world, including the thirteenth floor of a high-rise building in Hong Kong. The balcony where the unit was installed is only 3 x 5 feet. So the system can be used almost anywhere.

Right now, northern Iraqis and Syrians have to rely on places like Turkey to obtain their food while they face conflict with ISIS. Aquaponics systems are helping to alleviate this need. Iraqi minorities that have been displaced by ISIS will be trained to grow food for themselves, even in a nomadic or mobile environment. This will provide food for the long term.

Phase one continues with BTJ missionaries providing emergency items that are desperately needed. The missionaries are able to serve Iraqi and Syrian unreached people groups with the humanitarian aid they need to get back on their feet. Back to Jerusalem missionaries have also tackled the long-term question of how to provide aid without creating dependency.

Phase Two: Providing Missionaries and Gospel Materials

After meeting physical needs outlined in Phase One, BTJ missionaries focus on phase two: the long process of helping people work through the spiritual and emotional trauma they have experienced. The aftereffects of rape, murder, and poverty can be deadly if people have no emotional and/or spiritual support. The refugee camps are in desperate need of Christian materials and people to present those materials. The camps are full of people suffering from loss and depression. Missionaries and Bible materials in the local language provide a healing message for them.

Historically, many of the unreached people groups have restricted their contact with outside groups and have remained homogenous for generations; this has kept them from being exposed to the gospel. But these people groups are now on the run to escape the persecution of ISIS. They are disoriented, dispersed, and more vulnerable to outside influences than ever before. For the first time in long time, these unreached people groups are accessible to the gospel. Parents have lost children, and children have lost parents. Only the name of Jesus can heal their hurt, pain, and loss.

Furthermore, most of the children are not able to attend school. Even the schools for locals in Iraq and Syria have been suspended because of the influx of refugee children. So, the children have no activities to participate in at all. The villages that BTJ is working in do not even have balls for children to kick around. Back to Jerusalem provides children with materials and activities to share the gospel. It also runs a program called DOVE—the first children's program of its kind—which was created, produced, and distributed in China. Developed in early 2000s, DOVE equips more than 250,000 Sunday school trainers to share the gospel. Each of these Sunday school trainers commits to train an additional ten Sunday school teachers.

Because of the success of DOVE in China, Chinese churches have sent representatives to train others in the Philippines, India, Mongolia, Vietnam, Pakistan, Ethiopia, Egypt, Norway, Finland, and Sweden.

Now, due to the needs of thousands of children in Iraq, Chinese underground churches are sending DOVE trainers to Iraq to share the good news. The children in the refugee villages have nothing else going on. They spend all day reliving their traumatic experiences and trying to digest the ugly truth that they have been forced to live with. But the efforts of the Chinese involve constructive and proven methods to help young children deal with emotional pain.

Back to Jerusalem provides videos, audio players, booklets, and Bibles to refugees to share the love of Christ with the many unreached minorities of Iraq and Syria. Out of the most horrible situation, BTJ missionaries have provided a small window of hope, a once-in-a-lifetime opportunity, to refugees. What the devil meant for a stumbling block has perhaps become a spiritual stepping-stone for several different people groups.

Phase Three: Bringing the Gospel to ISIS

I have worked in China, Burma, Vietnam, North Korea, Iran, Sudan, and other nations, and I admit that phase three is the boldest measure of presenting the gospel that I have ever been a part of.

Pastor Joshua is an underground church pastor from China and is one of the main "uncles" of the "No Name" network of several million believers. This network tries to remain as inconspicuous as possible because it is illegal in China.

Pastor Joshua and I sat in a Chinese restaurant in Phnom Penh, Cambodia. "You're going to Iraq?" asked Pastor Joshua. "Yes, well, we are working in the refugee camps where many of the Iraqis have fled," I said, referring to the camps in Turkey.

In the beginning weeks after the ISIS attack, Turkey was still relatively secure, and many of the refugees were pouring over its border.

Pastor Joshua wanted to go with me. We have been working together closely for many years. We have traveled throughout the Middle East to countries like Dubai and Iran. We have traveled to Cambodia, Vietnam, Laos, the Philippines, and North Korea. I was with him when he was mugged for the first time in Uganda on our way to Sudan. I can even remember his first trip to America and the time when he drank thick, white sausage gravy to quench his thirst instead of pouring it over his dry biscuits. He is my closest colleague in China and has been one of my best friends for many years. We rarely work apart from each other.

Though he wanted to accompany me to Turkey, Joshua was unable to go because he was training a team of about twenty BTJ missionaries from China in Cambodia's capital.

Joshua is one of the most important strategists for the Chinese BTJ vision. He has several training schools throughout China and is directly involved in the recruiting, training, and sending out of Chinese missionaries in his network.

Joshua has funding from both Chinese and the South Korean businessmen who are working and running businesses in China. He has an almost endless supply of young, spiritually hungry, sold-out missionaries from the various underground churches in China, and he has had the unique experience of suffering for his faith. He has been beaten for preaching the gospel of Jesus Christ, and he has been sent to prison several times. Few things can prepare a person for the challenges of the mission field like being beaten until you prefer to die, only to survive by the grace of God.

"Isn't it dangerous?" Joshua asked in his kind, fatherly way. He is always looking out for me and trying to keep me safe, as good friends do.

"That is what they tell me, but I have to go. There are so many Christians who are dying for the name of Jesus. ISIS is killing everyone in its path. There are so many people there who need our help." In Cambodia, I could talk freely and as loudly as I wanted because there probably weren't any people in the restaurant who could understand our conversation in Chinese.

"How are you going to lead them to Jesus?" Joshua immediately asked. I could always count on him to keep things simple and straight to the point. He has a one-track mind. He is always looking to lead people to Jesus. Everything he does leads back to that one aim.

Even when he was beaten, thrown into prison, and threatened with death if he did not keep his mouth shut, Joshua did not stop sharing about Jesus. Joshua would not stop because he could not stop. I have known him for almost half my life, and he has never kept his mouth shut about the goodness of Jesus.

Many people falsely think that the term "underground church" implies a secret society of Chinese Christians who hide their faith so that others will not know that they are Christians, and who practice Christianity only in the privacy of a secret closet or room. Nothing could be further from the truth.

Chinese Christians like Pastor Joshua burn with an unexplainable fire to share their relationship with Jesus with others, no matter what the consequences. The term "underground" refers to the legality of the fellowship. The churches have to meet in unregistered locations because the government refuses to officially recognize them.

In response to his question, I said, "Well, right now, our main focus is to help them survive. They do not have food, water, or shelter. They need so much right now. Honestly, I do not even know where to start."

"Do we have a plan to bring them Bibles?"

"Not yet," I admitted. "We just started, so I am not sure what we can do and what we can't do."

"What about ISIS?" Joshua asked.

"Oh, they are evil. They are just plain evil. They are killing people, raping women, beheading Christians. I can't even describe it. Have you seen the news?"

Joshua just shook his head. He had been so deeply involved in the work in Cambodia for the last several months that he had not been able to sit and watch the news about what was going on in the rest of the world. "We need to share Jesus with them," he said.

Joshua may have more people in his church than the entire population of Norway, but, honestly, he could be so beautifully ignorant sometimes.

He did not give me much time to think about his statement before he added, "Are the members of ISIS any different from the apostle Paul? Didn't Jesus die for them, as well?"

I grabbed a large chunk of chicken with my chopsticks and stuffed it into my mouth. I needed a moment to think about Joshua's words, and I think better when my mouth is preoccupied with chewing food and I am prohibited from speaking.

When I went to my room that night, I was unable to sleep. Who was ISIS? I had thought of ISIS militants in the way that the newspapers had described them. Actually, that's false, because I don't read newspapers anymore, and neither does most of the world; but the point is that the mainstream news media wanted me to believe that ISIS was the evil boogeyman hiding under my bed. Every CNN report, BBC investigation, or Web site news source reported on the evil nature of ISIS.

Each time I had heard about ISIS, the hate in my heart toward them had grown deeper and deeper. I would be lying if I said that I hadn't felt an urge to abandon my evangelistic endeavors for a season and rejoin my marine buddies to go blast some jihadists to kingdom come.

But Joshua's words echoed in my head. And the words of Ephesians 6:12–13 came to mind:

> *For we do not wrestle against flesh and blood, but against the rulers, against the authorities, against the cosmic powers over this present darkness, against the spiritual forces of evil in the heavenly places. Therefore take up the whole armor of God, that you may be able to withstand in the evil day, and having done all, to stand firm.*

This message was later echoed by our Amish friends. ISIS was not the enemy. They were being controlled by the enemy.

Jesus died for the members of ISIS. His blood was shed for them. Is it too much to believe that the ISIS fighters have been deceived? Jesus loves them because He created them, and if He loves them, then am I not commanded to love them, too?

When I thought of all the killing, maiming, raping, and torturing that the terrorists had inflicted on so many people, I felt that it was impossible for me to love them. It seemed too big of a task. But if I were to kill them for being evil, keeping in mind that they had been deceived, then wouldn't I merely be killing the victim without addressing the main problem?

As I thought about these things, it occurred to me that ISIS was not the problem. The root problem was that they didn't know Jesus Christ. Instead of sending bombs and bullets, BTJ missionaries needed to send Bibles and missionaries.

That moment is when Phase Three was added to the BTJ vision for the relief efforts in Iraq and Syria.

Phase Three, Part One: The Gospel Cloud

Phase Three involves taking the gospel to ISIS. Instead of running from ISIS, BTJ was going to target ISIS. The group would no longer be in our rearview mirror; instead, it would be in our crosshairs.

Back to Jerusalem has invented a new device that it has been secretly using and testing in Iran. It is called the Gospel Cloud. It is our "nuclear" option. We plan to take this weapon into the enemy's camp. Because of the nature of the device, I am not able to show a picture of it. But this is how it works.

The Gospel Cloud unit is a small mobile device, the size of a mobile phone, that missionaries can easily carry in their pocket. It sends out a Wi-Fi signal; but instead of connecting users to the Internet, it acts as its very own server, and it only allows the user to access a Web page that has been designed specifically for them. It sends out wireless signals that extend roughly one hundred meters. Anyone with a mobile phone, laptop, iPad, tablet, and so forth, can receive the wireless signal and sign on. Remember, ISIS is one of the most technologically advanced terrorists groups in the history of the world. Many of their members carry electronic devices with them, and we plan to use this to our advantage.

The Wi-Fi connection can be easily detected and allows a person who is close enough to the Gospel Cloud to sign on anytime. The hope is that, when ISIS members are on a bus, a train, in the remote desert, or at a cafe, they will see the free Wi-Fi and sign on.

They will believe they are on the Internet, but they will not be. When they open the browser and type in "www.google.com" or "www.youtube.com," they will be directed to our own Web site that we have created just for them. Again, the user does not really know that he or she is not connected to the Internet, because the device simulates the experience of surfing.

Our Web site has a home page that offers free movies, music, and e-books for instant download, or they can be streamed directly from our site. To fully understand this concept, think of what you encounter when you first sign on to the Internet at a hotel or an airport. First you are taken to a portal page where you must agree to some terms and conditions or watch some advertisements before you can sign on and explore the Internet. The Gospel Cloud is the same experience, except that the user never really leaves that page. He or she navigates only deeper and deeper into it.

ISIS members can browse through the Web pages of content and download a free Bible in their language, or free Christian music, or even Christian movies that teach about Jesus. If, at any time, they do not like it, they can sign off.

The good thing about being in the middle of the desert is that there are not a lot of Wi-Fi options competing with the Gospel Cloud. Boredom is in our favor. Back to Jerusalem will soon have a monopoly on free Wi-Fi connections in the middle of nowhere.

The Gospel Cloud is battery operated, so the missionary can actually set it up in strategic locations or in the middle of the desert in a tree or under a fake rock that we create. Then it can be retrieved at a later time.

We also have solar units that will allow us to strategically place the Gospel Cloud throughout ISIS-controlled territories and provide continuous saturated coverage of the gospel message!

Because the Gospel Cloud is not really connected to the Internet, it cannot be stopped or controlled. Our content cannot be blocked by the government or by ISIS.

In addition to this, we have added a bonus feature that is particularly exciting for Chinese BTJ missionaries. There is a box on the home page that allows missionaries to anonymously chat with ISIS members. When the members sign on, they will find a little box in which they can ask questions or become engaged with a missionary whose identity and location remain anonymous. That means that a female believer from China can chat with a male ISIS member in a completely safe environment, without revealing her identity and without the ISIS member discovering that he is being evangelized by a woman.

Because we have invented this little tool, it will be very difficult for ISIS to find it or to stop it. They cannot stop what they do not know.

Phase Three sounds completely insane to those who do not understand the power of the gospel. The Bible says, "*God chose what is foolish in the world to shame the wise; God chose what is weak in the world to shame the strong*" (1 Corinthians 1:27).

How can seemingly abstract love combat tangible evil? Just allowing that idea to be translated into the form of words on a page makes me feel foolish and instantly invokes in my mind images of hippies stuffing flowers into the rifle barrels of riot-control police.

Yet, as silly as it sounds, I have been persuaded that the very same ISIS jihadists who are selling innocent children in an open sex-slave market were created in the image of God. God's image in their lives has been obscured by sin, but it is still there.

The Bible teaches that, outside of the blood of Jesus, I am no better than the worst jihadist of ISIS. Jesus taught that when someone thinks evil thoughts in his or her mind, that person has already sinned. (See Matthew 5:21–22, 28.) According to the measuring stick of righteousness that Jesus introduced, I have been a murderer, a blasphemer, an adulterer, a liar, and a thief before breakfast some days, and those are the sins I am willing to admit on paper. I would not whisper most of the evils that I have entertained in my own mind in an empty room by myself with the lights off. The sins I've committed in my thoughts are just as bad, and at times worse, than those of ISIS.

However, deep down within me is the image of God. Being made in the image of God does not mean merely that we resemble

Him but that we are like Him. We have inherited His characteristics. The ideas and concepts of justice, love, affection, desire, and creativity are all attributes that we have inherited from our Creator. He is in our DNA. These characteristics of God in our lives may not always be apparent, but they still exist under the thick, crusty layers of sin, having the power to convict us. The same is true for the members of ISIS.

Paul wrote,

> *For as many as have sinned without law shall also perish without law: and as many as have sinned in the law shall be judged by the law; (for not the hearers of the law are just before God, but the doers of the law shall be justified. For when Gentiles, which have not the law, do by nature the things contained in the law, these, having not the law, are a law unto themselves: which show the work of the law written in their hearts, their conscience also bearing witness, and their thoughts the mean while accusing or else excusing one another;) in the day when God shall judge the secrets of men by Jesus Christ according to my gospel.* (Romans 2:12–16 KJV)

All people have their beginning in God. He is the Giver of life, and no matter how far we roam from Him, His almighty fingerprint is always upon our hearts. He is not fully revealed through our feeble flesh, but His image is residual in us because we are His creation. That is why I believe that the most radical ISIS jihadists cannot kill and rape people without the pain of God's hurt and disappointment surfacing somewhere in their hearts. We often refer to this awareness as the human conscience, but Paul describes it as the law of God written upon the hearts of man. (See Romans 2:15.)

All humans have been branded with the law of God. Though some members of ISIS are like the Egyptian pharaoh in the book of Exodus, having given their hardened hearts completely over to their desires, others have merely been deceived.

This means that when a member of ISIS rapes a little child, kills an innocent mother, or cuts off the head of a peaceful Christian for the first time, something inside of him screams out, "This is not right!"

He may not know why it is wrong, but something inside of him will wrestle with the merits of killing innocent people, stealing from poor families, and persecuting the weakest members of society. He may search the Koran for answers, because that is the only book he has access to, but he will not find the answers there.

We believe that this is when tools like the Gospel Cloud will come into play. When ISIS members sign on to the free Wi-Fi provided by BTJ, they will see the story of Jesus and receive the answers that they seek—often, for the first time. Then the Holy Spirit will continue to work in their hearts, confirming many things that have been challenging them. The answers will not be a new revelation as much as they will be a confirmation of the things that the Holy Spirit has already been speaking to them.

What if an ISIS member who fights for Islam with the same type of passion the Apostle Paul had when he persecuted the first-century church were to come to Christ? What if the zeal and passion of the hatred in his life were turned around to become a passion to reach the lost in the land between the walls?

That is why Phase Three is so important. Fighting ISIS with a fire on fire type of battle will not provide a long-term solution to the problem. The end of violence and the road to long-term peace are possible only through Jesus Christ. Every other route is a waste of time. Only the love of Christ can fully conquer the hate of ISIS and wipe away the scars and the pain.

How Bibles and Christian evangelistic tools will get into the areas of ISIS is a matter of an evolving strategy that we are working on. The Gospel Cloud unit is essential to Phase Three of the BTJ mission, but it is not the only part of Phase Three. Let's now turn our attention to another method of bringing the gospel to ISIS.

Phase Three, Part Two: Business as Mission

Another method of getting the gospel into ISIS territory is through business. ISIS is still trading and conducting business. In fact, it has even started to create its own currency and to mint its own coins. This is an opportunity for BTJ, because few cultures in the world do business better than the Chinese.

Underground Chinese Christians who are being sent to Iraq and Syria are not supported by foreign embassies, and they will have no diplomatic support from China if they are captured by ISIS for preaching the good news of Jesus Christ. However, they believe that Jesus is the only answer to deal with the ISIS threat and that the mission is worth the sacrifice.

Chinese missionaries are also focusing on doing what they do best—starting small businesses. Unlike the Western Christian mission model, which requires continual funding from the sending church body, the Chinese are going with very little funds and support. In order to survive on the mission field in Syria and Iraq, they must work as the first-century missionaries did during the days of Paul. They must become "*tentmakers*" (Acts 18:3).

The Chinese church understands that long-term missions in the land between the walls cannot be done without the sustainability of a job, which requires a skill or a trade. In order to multiply and send out as many missionaries as possible, the Chinese have adopted a new approach. Business as Mission, or BAM, has emerged as a significant new model for mission work around the world. It is quickly becoming the "Coca-Cola" of Christian terminology in mission conferences.

Today's globalized economy has created strategic opportunities for Christian businesses in some of the most unlikely corners of the world, including areas that are controlled by ISIS. ISIS can fight secularization, but it will lose any battle against globalization if it intends to move the oil it has confiscated and to continue to be on the cutting edge of technology with its YouTube videos.

Business as Mission is a relatively new term but is based on biblical concepts. Other expressions used for BAM include "transformational business," "tentmaking," "great commission company," and "kingdom business." These are very generic terms, but the way they are used among the Chinese in the BTJ context is usually different from the way they are used by the Western church, and it is important to clarify the differences.

In the Back to Jerusalem vision, BAM is a means to an end; it is not the main focus, meaning that missions is the primary focus and business is the secondary focus, not the other way around. However, as it is used and taught today in mainstream Christian curriculum, BAM is business with a ministry component. The phrase "Let's keep business, business" (meaning, "Let's keep business and ministry separate") is often used. Even in missionary circles, you will hear people say that business and missions need to be kept separate. I understand what they are saying, but this policy may be a fatal error for people who are mission-focused in an area controlled by ISIS.

Back to Jerusalem is mission-focused. Our vision of sharing the gospel of Jesus Christ drives everything, including our businesses.

The dichotomy between sacred and secular does not exist in Back to Jerusalem's BAM. We believe it is a false dichotomy that has, in fact, deeply affected people's views on work, business, church, and missions. Back to Jerusalem missionaries do not share the idea that religion and faith need to be quarantined from other aspects of life. If we look at the Bible, we see amazing examples of businessmen, kings, leaders, judges, crop owners, and soldiers who interconnect every aspect of their lives with the will of the Father. Life is not like a series of boxes that must remain separated but instead like a ball of interconnected wires that all have a single purpose.

BAM is a part of a large global movement in the Chinese underground house church that recognizes and responds to God's call to take the gospel of Jesus Christ to the whole world, even to the parts that don't want it. Chinese missionaries are not the first missionaries to use BAM. Back to Jerusalem is not even the first group to use the title Business as Mission. In fact, many groups that note the way in which we use the term will probably be upset because they will feel that the BTJ terminology is polluting the purity of BAM. But the Chinese applications of BAM are unique and will vary from country to country, business to business, and network to network.

To get an idea of the international or mainstream Christian view of BAM, and how it is different from the underground Chinese view, here is a quote from an article that appeared in the *Lausanne World Pulse*:

> Unfortunately there is sometimes a confusing misuse of the term BAM. Let's be clear: BAM is not "Business for Mission," a fundraising activity facilitated by the profits generated by business. Neither is BAM "Business as Platform" (i.e., an attempt to obtain visas to do "real ministry"). Rather, genuine BAM is the practice of business as a calling and ministry in its own right—a manifestation of the Kingdom of God.[159]

Respected academic religious institutions have embraced BAM as it is defined above. However, the author of the article admitted that BAM as it is taught and defined by the Western world has a hard time being effective in the 10/40 Window.

> One of the biggest hurdles for BAM businesses around the world, especially in and around the so-called "10/40 Window," is securing investment capital. BAM is not built on traditional models of charitable fundraising and donations, but upon a foundation of the disciplined allocation and return of capital.
>
> One of the biggest challenges for the global BAM movement is the lack of BAM investment funds—capital managed with vision, professionalism, excellence, and integrity.[160]

It is hard to garner investors in an environment that does not promise much return on investment. In order to make a legitimate forecast for investors, a business needs a stable environment, a functional government, investment security, and so forth.

ISIS has not controlled portions of Syria and Iraq for very long. A business plan for an area controlled by ISIS or on the border of ISIS would not last a week past its registration (assuming there was a way to register it), because the situation in that region changes on a daily basis. Such a scenario scares the living tar out of investors who want to make as much return on their investment as possible.

To BTJ Chinese missionaries who are doing business in the land between the walls, BAM refers to any use of business that advances the gospel of Jesus Christ in a long-term, sustainable way. For Back to Jerusalem, BAM is not a term that has been developed as a result of years of research, study, and analysis. Instead, it is a practical term. BAM is being implemented throughout the land between the walls as part of a new trend that is becoming more and more common as the number of Christians in China increases.

Chinese missionaries have set up businesses in Tibet, North Korea, Cambodia, South Sudan, Iran, and Syria, as well as on the border of Afghanistan and Pakistan. Their business as mission model is unique and provides a natural inroad into these communities to share the good news.

We have noted that those who teach BAM in the traditional way admit that one of the problems they face is the lack of financial capital in businesses in the 10/40 Window. No kidding! Legitimate businesses that focus on financial returns have to evaluate the risk and capital involved in investments before committing to them. Iraq is one of the most volatile regions in the world right now. Good luck trying to find a stable business model to present at a board meeting of investors that insures capital in war-torn Syria.

However, BTJ is a part of a new business trend in Asia in which legitimate businesses are willing to invest in and take a risk on mission projects—that is, mission projects using business not for a return on financial investment but because they are viable mission opportunities. Many businesses in Indonesia, the Philippines, Malaysia, Vietnam, Laos, Sri Lanka, and other nations are run by overseas Chinese. These Chinese carry the passports of their current country and often love their homeland very much, but they still feel a strong connection with the lands of their ancestors. They have heard about the BTJ vision, and they are sold out to it. They want to support it and be a part of it. They may not understand missions, but they understand business, and they clearly understand the relational inroads that business can make, such as bonding and making a difference for Jesus Christ.

Anyone familiar with the narrow shopping streets of China knows that the storefronts contain all the goods, but there are also bedrooms in the back of the buildings. Family time and meals all take place around the family business or businesses. Chinese very rarely have only one job. They are entrepreneurs in the real sense of the word, exploring many opportunities at the same time.

The Chinese businessmen fit right into the business environment in Iraq and Syria. Like the tribes of ISIS-controlled territory, they have a collective identity. To best understand that collective identity, consider how the Chinese eat.

When Westerners sit down at a restaurant, they each obtain their own menus, decide what sounds good to them, and order food. When the meal comes, each person eats his or her own meal. This is not the way it is done in China or in a tribal community. In China, one menu comes to the table, one person decides what everyone will eat, and, when the food arrives, everyone shares it.

This collective identity directly relates to Chinese business and the Chinese BTJ vision for Iraq and Syria. The Chinese plan is to use business to set up sustainable mission stations around Iraq. This will enable the missionaries to create a positive cash flow that will sustain their long-term residence in ISIS-controlled areas.

Remember, these Chinese are not normal missionaries trained in seminaries and elite Bible schools; they are uneducated farmers and street vendors who currently operate in marketplaces around the world. Their church services often take place in factories, office cubicles, and closed shops. They are not involved in a full-time ministry sustained by writing monthly letters to donors to give updates about their progress. Back to Jerusalem missionaries have cut their teeth on the hardships of life as they occur on the streets. They have a heart to take the gospel out into the streets, but they still have a responsibility to put rice on the table.

So, Back to Jerusalem's concept of BAM is not a strategy that was conceived by great leaders who congregated together to discover a methodology to effectively proselytize the 10/40 Window.

It is merely the best term that can be used to identify the work of BTJ missionaries in business without restricting their actions with definitions.

The businesses that BTJ uses blend with the environment; this is easy, since almost everything in the world is made in China. This puts China at the top of the map when vendors or merchants are doing international business. Often, the Chinese are not thought of as being evangelists, so this makes them even less of a target for ISIS.

Small-time entrepreneurs from China are also not famous for coming to the table with a lot of credit or official bank transfers on hand. Usually the Chinese just show up like their countrymen did during the days of the Wild West in America—sleeves rolled up, full of hope, and willing to outwork anyone around them for less pay than the cheapest laborer.

Setting up businesses in ISIS-controlled areas may sound impossible, but remember that ISIS is the wealthiest terrorist organization in the world. It has televisions, mobile phones, earphones, routers, cameras, cars, shoes, watches, socks, furniture, alarm systems, and so on. Where do you think they buy their goods? Like most everyone else, they buy them from China. The goal of the underground house church is to provide the supplies that ISIS needs by way of a Chinese businessman who has other things in mind than merely making money.

TWELVE

Can God Reach ISIS?

The gospel message will not appear in Iraq "accidentally" and then coincidently slip into the hands of ISIS members, converting radical jihadists. Missionaries, Bibles, and Christian resources must be sent without delay. Every day that the gospel message is delayed in Iraq is a day when evil is imposed upon the weakest and most vulnerable citizens in Iraq and Syria.

Chinese missionaries who go to Iraq have a seemingly insurmountable task, but they are not starting from scratch. The identity of the Creator was stamped upon the hearts of the members of ISIS before they were even born, and nothing they do can make God stop pursuing them with His love.

The idea that Iraq and Syria are too dangerous to go to and that ISIS fighters are too evil to receive Jesus' forgiveness is contrary to the gospel message. Who is the message of the gospel intended for if not for the lost and the frightened? How weak is the belief of Christians who believe that they can evangelize only from within the borders of stable, free countries? What if, as was argued earlier, the stability and freedom of countries and peoples comes only after the evangelization of a society, and not before it?

What, then, shall we say is the urgency of our mission? Let me repeat that Chinese BTJ missionaries believe that the gospel message has been woven into the fabric of the heart of every member of ISIS. The terrorists' passion for Islam is a misguided fervor in their DNA to serve something greater than themselves.

There is no doubt that ISIS must be stopped. The organization must be defeated and destroyed. The evil acts that they are perpetrating must end, but the weapons of this carnal world cannot stand against the power of Islam. Islam is a spirit that will overpower humanism and subdue secularism. Socially embraced atheism mixed with the spiritual apathy of the church leaves spiritual voids that must be filled. Nature demands it. After all that we have seen ISIS members do, knowing the atrocities they are capable of, is it possible for us to ever see them as victims in a spiritual battle?

ISIS can and will be defeated. My hope is that this book will help readers understand a terrorist organization that will one day be found only in the record of history, and that those who pick up this book in ten or twenty years will read about a group that no longer exists.

The state of affairs in Iraq and Syria is causing large numbers of Muslims to question their faith, possibly more than ever before. And what ISIS has intended as a way to cleanse the region has often had the opposite effect. Yazidi minorities who have come face-to-face with the evils of Islam are arriving at the conclusion that their indigenous religion is not providing them with much comfort in their distress, but that there is something different about Christianity.

Christian convert Shamo, in an interview with CBN News, said, "I can say only one word about the difference between Islam and Christianity. The difference is between earth and sky and heaven. We are thinking every day why we are not behaving like Christians...We really saw a real humanity in their life."[161]

Shamo was born a Yazidi and has suffered the impact of extreme Islam. "Please, either if you can protect us, provide us an international protection, or take us out of the country because we don't want to give our women and our children anymore. And please pray for the Yazidi people to come to Christ just like me."

I saw a similar yearning in the Yazidi refugee area I worked in.

"I am a Christian," I would often say to the Yazidi refugees. Though I did not want to offend them, I would often ask if I could pray for them. I could not walk away without praying for them. How could I walk away from a drowning man with a lifesaving floatation device in my hand?

I often said, "We Christians love all of the Yazidi people. We have seen your pain and suffering, and we just want you to know that we want to help in any way that we can and that we are praying for you. Would it be okay if I pray for you?"

The Yazidi people, who have been unreached for generations, never turned me away when I offered to pray for them.

There are reports of indigenous Christian workers who have, against their better judgment, decided to stay behind in Mosul because they felt that there was a unique opportunity to share the love of Christ. "I think of the [indigenous Christian] workers who stayed behind in Mosul and the surrounding areas because there are so many who are receptive to the Gospel. They are willing to risk being in an area under the rule of ISIS for the privilege of more and more fruit for Christ," said the Christian Aid Mission's Middle East director.[162]

There are unconfirmed rumors circulating of small resistance groups that are forming in the occupied territories of ISIS. These groups are much too small to resist ISIS openly; but, if the rumors are true, they are growing.

Back to Jerusalem missionaries from China are very familiar with the framework needed to work in small groups and the importance of underground networks. Their ideas and experience of working in closed environments could be a tremendous resource for new Iraqi believers. If there is an underground network of Christians, then Bibles, audio Bibles, Christian books, videos, and so forth can be distributed in a much more effective way.

Back to Jerusalem missionaries from China show the universality of the gospel message in the very fact that they, too, are Christians. Very few Arabs, Yazidis, Kurds, or Persians expect Chinese to be Christian. All too often, Christianity is considered to be a European religion when, in reality, Jesus most likely would have looked more like Osama bin Laden than a white-skinned, blond-haired, blue-eyed European. The customs of Jesus were also more similar to the eastern Asian customs of the Chinese than to those of the European culture.

ISIS is not prepared for that. They are not ready for Chinese Christians to share Jesus in Syria or Iraq. The Chinese have been labeled as Daoists, Confucionists, Buddhists, and atheists, but never as Christians, so the Back to Jerusalem teams will take the enemy by surprise.

Critics will, of course, point out the many shortcomings of the Chinese in the Middle East environment. Chinese missionaries are certain to meet many challenges that evangelists from other nations would not face; but from the testing fires of Chinese persecution, the missionaries have the potential to show the loving nature of Father God from experience. The Chinese will be able to reflect on their own testimonies of hardship and persecution and share how God changed their lives.

Unlike the angry Allah, who is so central in the Koran, Jesus Christ is full of compassion and wants to have a relationship with us. Unlike the constant displeasure of Allah, whose love for his people is never mentioned in the Koran, our Father God loves us, and His love is the central theme of the Bible. The Chinese missionaries can introduce the refugees to this loving Father.

Unlike the Arabic Koran, the Bible can be presented to people in ISIS-controlled territory in their mother tongue. The non-Arabic-speaking minorities in ISIS-controlled territory will never have a deep connection to the Koran, which is made available to them only in the Arabic language. It is absolutely impossible for the daily prayers of the mosque to ever reach the core of their lives because these prayers are not in their mother tongue. The lack of connection between these words and their meanings will become more and more evident when people groups controlled by ISIS hear the gospel message for the first time in their own mother tongue.

As mentioned earlier, Brother Yun is one of the most well-known Chinese Christians in the world today. He is one of the main representatives of the Back to Jerusalem vision of the Chinese church. On November 17, 2014, in a church outside Sydney, Australia, he shared about the things that were happening with ISIS and how zealous believers from his home country were making the effort to reach out to them. As he came to the conclusion of his message, he said,

> There are millions of people that have never held a Bible in their hands. God told me, "When I set you free from this prison in China, you must remember that there are so many people in this world who live in different kinds of prisons, and they still must be set free with My power."
>
> I have a dream, a heavenly dream, that, one day, every Muslim believer will have the living Word of God in their hands. I fully believe that the Bible had the power to change my life, as well as millions of other Chinese, and I firmly believe that the Bible can transform the Islamic world, as well.
>
> God is opening a door for the gospel of Jesus Christ. He has opened a back door to the Middle East for thousands of Chinese to enter in with the gospel message.

I just left Brisbane, where I had a meeting only two hundred meters from the G20 summit on November 16, and I was praying for them and their meetings. As we were worshiping the Lord, I saw a vision of a major celestial meeting taking place over them, strategizing how the gospel can be made available to every people group in the world. The book of Isaiah, chapter 6 says, *"In the year that King Uzziah died I saw the Lord sitting upon a throne, high and lifted up; and the train of his robe filled the temple.... And I heard the voice of the Lord saying, 'Whom shall I send, and who will go for us?' Then I said, 'Here I am! Send me.'"*

At the same time that the G20 nations were working to solve the financial and security problems of the earth, I saw the heavenly beings come together and say that this is our opportunity. Let's increase the kingdom of God throughout the world.

The Lord wants to send you. How many are willing to go?

I know that you have your own plans and visions in your life, but the Lord has not forgotten the city of Nineveh. He has not forsaken the refugees in Turkey, Syria, and Iraq.

How many people here have more than one Bible at home? If you have more than one, I challenge you to have a bit more compassion and think about those who have never had access to the Word of God.

You might say that you are too old, but maybe you can speak to the leadership of your church to encourage an uprising—an uprising to support the efforts of the Chinese in the Middle East.

There are also many refugees who are living in Western countries. You have the opportunity to reach them.

ISIS is not the Lord. There is only one Lord, and His name is Jesus! The very same Jesus said, "*All authority in heaven and on earth has been given to me. Go therefore and make disciples of all nations.*"

Do you want to be a disciple of Jesus Christ? Think about this strongly before you commit. Stand up and ask the Lord to use you and say to yourself, "I want to follow Jesus."

How will you respond to the threat of ISIS? Will you help to alleviate one of the largest man-made humanitarian disasters in the world today? Will you support the brave Chinese missionaries living and ministering in the 10/40 window? Will you pray for the perpetrators, the victims, and the refugees of terrorism alike and share the gospel of peace and forgiveness with them?

> *You have heard that it was said, "You shall love your neighbor and hate your enemy." But I say to you, Love your enemies and pray for those who persecute you, so that you may be sons of your Father who is in heaven.* (Matthew 5:43–45)

To learn how to help, please visit www.backtojerusalem.com.

Notes

Preface

1. "Back to Jerusalem is the goal of the Chinese church to evangelize the unreached peoples from eastern provinces of China, westwards towards Jerusalem." For more information, visit www.backtojerusalem.com.

Chapter One

2. Sasha Goldstein, James Warren, and Bill Hutchinson, "ISIS Militants Behead Abducted American Journalist James Wright Foley in Graphic Video," *New York Daily News*, August 19, 2014.

3. Patrick Goodenough, "Mother of Beheaded American Journalist Urges ISIS to Spare Other Captives," CNSNews.com (Cybercast News Service), August 19, 2014, http://cnsnews.com/news/article/patrick-goodenough/mother-beheaded-american-journalist-urges-isis-spare-other-captives.

4. Maria Abi-Habib, "Assad Policies Aided Rise of Islamic State Militant Group," *Wall Street Journal*, August 22, 2014, http://online.wsj.com/articles/assad-policies-aided-rise-of-islamic-state-militant-group-1408739733.

5. Charles River Editors, *The Islamic State of Iraq and Syria: The History of ISIS/ISIL* (CreateSpace, 2014), 45.

6. A caliphate is a dominion that is ruled by an Islamic religious and political leader called a *caliph*.

7. Amy Davidson, "Obama to Iraq: Your Problem Now," *New Yorker*, June 13, 2014, http://www.newyorker.com/news/amy-davidson/obama-to-iraq-your-problem-now.

8. Chelsea Carter, Catherine E. Shoichet, and Hambi Alkhshali, "Obama on ISIS in Syria: 'We Don't Have a Strategy Yet," CNN, September 4, 2014, http://www.cnn.com/2014/08/28/world/meast/isis-iraq-syria/.

9. Andre Walker, "More Brits Joined Jihad Than Volunteered for UK Army Reserves," Breitbart News Network, June 17, 2014, http://www.breitbart.com/Breitbart-London/2014/06/17/More-Brits-Sign-Up-For-ISIS-Than-Signed-Up-For-Army-Reserve.

10. Terrence McCoy, "How ISIS Leader Abu Bakr al-Baghdadi Became the World's Most Powerful Jihadi Leader," *Washington Post*, June 11, 2014, http://www.washingtonpost.com/news/morning-mix/wp/2014/06/11/how-isis-leader-abu-bakr-al-baghdadi-became-the-worlds-most-powerful-jihadi-leader/.

11. Aaron Y. Zelin, "Abu Bakr al-Baghdadi: Islamic State's Driving Force," BBC News, July 30, 2014, http://www.bbc.com/news/world-middle-east-28560449.

12. Jenna McLaughlin, "Was Iraq's Top Terrorist Radicalized at a US-Run Prison?" *Mother Jones*, July 11, 2014, http://www.motherjones.com/politics/2014/07/was-camp-bucca-pressure-cooker-extremism.

13. http://edition.cnn.com/TRANSCRIPTS/1406/16/wolf.02.html.

14. Jenna McLaughlin, "Was Iraq's Top Terrorist Radicalized at a US-Run Prison?"

15. http://edition.cnn.com/TRANSCRIPTS/1406/16/wolf.02.html.

16. https://news.vice.com/video/islamic-state-member-warns-of-nyc-attack-in-exclusive-interview-the-canadian-jihadist.

17. Terrence McCoy, "How ISIS Leader Abu Bakr al-Baghdadi Became the World's Most Powerful Jihadi Leader."

18. The Arab Spring was a series of protests that erupted in the countries of Tunisia, Algeria, Jordan, Egypt, and Yemen, and was sparked by the Tunisian "burning man," Mohamed Bouazizi, who set himself on fire after being mistreated by Tunisian authorities.

Chapter Two

19. Mark Landler, "Secret Report Ordered by Obama Identified Potential Uprisings," *New York Times*, February 16, 2011, http://www.nytimes.com/2011/02/17/world/middleeast/17diplomacy.html.

20. Steven Lee Myers, "$1 Billion Is Pledged to Support Libya Rebels," *New York Times*, June 9, 2011, http://www.nytimes.com/2011/06/10/world/africa/10diplo.html.

21. Webster G. Tarpley, "Al Qaeda Commander of NATO's Bloody Reign of Terror in Tripoli Is the Monster Abdel Hakim Belhadj, aka Abdel Hakim al-Hasadi, Friend of Osama bin Laden, Former US POW, and Infamous Killer of US Soldiers in Afghanistan," Tarpley.net, August 27, 2011, http://tarpley.net/2011/08/27/al-qaeda-commander-of-natos-bloody-reign-of-terror-in-tripoli-is-the-monster-abdel-hakim-belhadj/.

22. Eric Schmitt, Helene Cooper, and Michael S. Schmidt, "Deadly Attack in Libya Was Major Blow to C.I.A. Efforts," *New York Times*, September 23, 2012, http://www.nytimes.com/2012/09/24/world/africa/attack-in-libya-was-major-blow-to-cia-efforts.html?pagewanted=all.

23. United Nations General Assembly, *Final Report of the Panel of Experts Established Pursuant to Resolution 1973 (2011) Concerning Libya*, S/2013/99,

March 9, 2013, 35, http://www.securitycouncilreport.org/atf/cf/%7B65BFCF9B-6D27-4E9C-8CD3-CF6E4FF96FF9%7D/s_2013_99.pdf.

24. Seymour M. Hersh, "The Red Line and the Rat Line," *London Review of Books*, vol. 36, no. 8 (2014): 21–24, http://www.lrb.co.uk/v36/n08/seymour-m-hersh/the-red-line-and-the-rat-line.

25. Miodrag Vojvodić, "Islamisti su razapinjali i na druge jezovite načine ubijali kršćane koji se nisu željeli odreći vjere," Bitno.net, April 21, 2014, http://www.bitno.net/vijesti/islamisti-su-razapinjali-na-druge-jezovite-nacine-ubijali-krscane-koji-se-nisu-zeljeli-odreci-vjere/#.U1-0F15bRZi.

26. See https://backtojerusalem.com/v3/2014/04/christians-hung-on-crosses-in-syria/.

27. See https://backtojerusalem.com/v3/2014/05/what-happens-to-this-man-who-denies-christ-is-unexpected/.

28. Richard Barrett, "Foreign Fighters in Syria," The Soufan Group, June 2014, 6.

29. Jim Sciutto, Jamie Crawford, and Chelsea J. Carter, "ISIS Can 'Muster' Between 20,000 and 31,500 Fighters, CIA Says," CNN, September 12, 2014, http://www.cnn.com/2014/09/11/world/meast/isis-syria-iraq/.

30. Dave Boyer, "Obama Administration Caught Off Guard by Islamist Threat in Iraq," *Washington Times*, August 13, 2014, http://www.washingtontimes.com/news/2014/aug/13/cia-director-2011-threat-islamic-caliphate-absurd/.

31. Aubrey Bailey, "Clear as Mud," letter to the editor, *Daily Mail*, September 5, 2014.

32. Graeme Wood, "What ISIS's Leader Really Wants," *New Republic*, September 1, 2014, http://www.newrepublic.com/article/119259/isis-history-islamic-states-newcaliphate-syria-and-iraq.

33. *Merriam-Webster's 11th Collegiate Dictionary*, s.v. "hadith."

34. "The Abbasid Dynasty: The Golden Age of Islamic Civilization," Saylor Foundation, History 101, Subunit 9.3.1, p.1, http://www.saylor.org/site/wp-content/uploads/2012/07/HIST101-9.3.1-AbbasidDynasty-FINAL.pdf.

35. Shafik Mandhai, "Muslim Leaders Reject Baghdadi's Caliphate," Al Jazeera, July 7, 2014, http://www.aljazeera.com/news/middleeast/2014/07/muslim-leaders-reject-baghdadi-caliphate-20147744058773906.html.

36. Mariam Karouny, "Apocalyptic Prophecies Drive Both Sides to Syrian Battle for End of Time," Reuters, April 1, 2014, http://www.reuters.com/article/2014/04/01/us-syria-crisis-prophecy-insightidUSBREA3013420140401.

Chapter Three

37. Nick Comming-Bruce, "5,500 Iraqis Killed Since Islamic State Began Its Military Drive, U.N. Says," *New York Times*, October 2, 2014, http://www.nytimes.com/2014/10/03/world/middleeast/un-reports-at-least-26000-civilian-casualties-in-iraq-conflict-this-year.html?_r=0.

38. Jung Chang and Jon Halliday, *Mao: The Unknown Story* (Great Britain: Jonathan Cape, 2005).

39. Robert Woodberry, *Christianity Today* 58, no.1 (2014). See also Andrea Palpant Dilley, "The Surprising Discovering About Those Colonialist, Proselytizing Missionaries," *Christianity Today* 58, no. 1 (2014).

40. Jake Tapper and Luis Martinez, "Bibles Destroyed in Afghanistan... By U.S. Military," ABC News, May 19, 2009), http://abcnews.go.com/blogs/politics/2009/05/bibles-destroye/.

41. "U.S. Military Says Afghan Bibles Have Been Destroyed," Reuters, May 5, 2009, http://in.reuters.com/article/2009/05/05/idINIndia-39421920090505.

Chapter Four

42. Seth Motel, "Young Americans Divided over Striking ISIS," Pew Research Center, September 17, 2014, http://www.pewresearch.org/fact-tank/2014/09/17/young-americans-divided-over-striking-isis/.

43. Peter McGraw and Joel Warner, "The Danish Cartoon Crisis of 2005 and 2006: 10 Things You Didn't Know About the Original Muhammad Controversy," *Huffington Post*, September 25, 2012, http://www.huffingtonpost.com/peter-mcgraw-and-joel-warner/muhammad-cartoons_b_1907545.html.

44. Ibn Ishaq, *The Life of Muhammad: A Translation of Ishaq's "Sirat Rasul Allah,"* ed. Abu Muhammad Abd al-Malik (Oxford, England: Oxford University Press, 1955), 146–148.

45. Richard A. Gabriel, *Muhammad: Islam's First Great General* (Norman, OK: University of Oklahoma Press, 2011), 81.

46. Richard A Gabriel, "The Warrior Project," *MHQ: The Quarterly Journal of Military History* 19, no. 4.

47. "Muhammad and...Jews of Medina," PBS, http://www.pbs.org/muhammad/ma_jews.shtml.

48. Koran 48:29, *The Koran*, ed. and trans. N. J. Dawood (Penguin Publishers, 1956, 1959, 1966, 1968, 1974, 1990, 1993, 1994, 1995, 1998, 2000).

49. Quoted in Robert Spencer, *The Truth About Muhammad: Founder of the World's Most Intolerant Religion* (Washington, D.C.: Regnery Publishing, 2006), 38.

50. Visit http://www.islamreview.com/articles/jihadholywarversesinthekoran.shtml for a complete list.

51. Gunnar Heinsohn and Daniel Pipes, "Arab-Israeli Fatalities Rank 49th," FrontPageMagazine.com, October 8, 2007, http://www.danielpipes.org/4990/arab-israelifatalities-rank-49th.

52. http://www.quran.com.

53. Robert Davis, "British Slaves on the Barbary Coast," http://www.bbc.co.uk/history/british/empire_seapower/white_slaves_01.shtml#top.

54. Frederic J. Frommer, "Ellison Uses Thomas Jefferson's Quran," Associated Press, January 5, 2007, http://www.washingtonpost.com/wp-dyn/content/article/2007/01/05/AR2007010500512.html.

55. Richard Zacks, *The Pirate Coast: Thomas Jefferson, the First Marines, and the Secret Mission of 1805* (New York: Hachette Books, 2005), 2.

56. Ibid., 4.

57. United States Department of State, *The Diplomatic Correspondence of the United States of America from the Signing of the Definitive Treaty of Peace* (Washington, D.C.: Blair & Rives, 1837), 605.

58. Mark Orwoll, "The World's Most Dangerous Countries," *Travel + Leisure*, August 2010, http://www.travelandleisure.com/articles/the-worlds-most-dangerous-countries.

59. "Malaysia," WordWatchList, http://www.worldwatchlist.ca/world-watch-list-countries/malaysia/.

60. Hanibal Goitom and the Global Legal Research Center, "Laws Criminalizing Apostasy in Selected Jurisdictions," The Law Library of Congress, May 2014, http://www.loc.gov/law/help/apostasy/index.php.

61. Max Fisher, "The Seven Countries Where the State Can Execute You for Being Atheist," *Washington Post*, December 10, 2012, http://www.loc.gov/law/help/apostasy/index.php#uae.

62. "UN Rights Experts Urge Saudi Arabia to Halt 'Stream of Executions, Beheadings,'" UN News Centre, September 9, 2014, http://www.un.org/apps/news/story.asp?NewsID=48672#.VKGAU14DnA.

63. https://www.youtube.com/watch?v=4CdR1Jd5wag.

64. http://www.trust.org/item/20130927165059-w9g0i/; http://www.cnn.com/2014/05/01/world/asia/brunei-sharia-law/.

Chapter Five

65. Daniel Williams, "Christianity in Iraq Is Finished," *Washington Post*, September 19, 2014, http://www.washingtonpost.com/opinions/christianity-in-iraq-is-finished/2014/09/19/21feaa7c-3f2f-11e4-b0ea-8141703bbf6f_story.html.

66. "It Happened First in Ancient Mesopotamia," The University of Chicago News Office (15 July 2013), http://www-news.uchicago.edu/releases/03/oi/030715.oi-firsts.shtml.

67. Patrick Cockburn, "Time Runs Out for Christian Iraq: ISIS Deadline Passes with Mass Flight," *Independent*, July 20, 2014, http://www.independent.co.uk/news/world/middle-east/time-runs-out-for-christian-iraq-isis-deadline-passes-with-mass-flight-9617606.html.

68. Shelby Lin Erdman, Mohammed Tawfeeq, and Hamdi Alkhshali, "Islamic Extremists Kill 270 in Attack on a Gas Field in Central Syria, Report Says,"

CNN, July 18, 2014, http://www.cnn.com/2014/07/18/world/meast/iraq-isis-christians-threatened/index.html?hpt=hp_t2.

69. Awr Hawkins, "ISIS Orders 'Jihad by Sex' for Unmarried Women," Breitbart News Network, July 8, 2014, http://www.breitbart.com/national-security/2014/07/08/isis-orders-jihad-by-sex-for-unmarried-women/.

70. Sam Greenhill, Jill Reilly, and Kieran Corcoran, "ISIS Butchers Leave 'Roads Lined with Decapitated Police and Soldiers': Battle for Baghdad Looms as Thousands Answer Iraqi Government's Call to Arms and Jihadists Bear Down on Capital," *Daily Mail*, June 2014, http://www.dailymail.co.uk/news/article-2655977/ISIS-militants-march-Baghdad-trademark-bullet-head-gets-way-control-north.html.

71. Jack Moore, "Mosul Seized: Jihadis Loot $429M from City's Central Bank to Make ISIS World's Richest Terror Force," *International Business Times*, June 11, 2014, http://www.ibtimes.co.uk/mosul-seized-jihadis-loot-429m-citys-central-bank-make-isis-worldsrichest-terror-force-1452190.

72. "Abraham," Jewish Encyclopedia Online, http://www.jewishencyclopedia.com/articles/360-abraham.

73. Eyder Peralta, "Video Shows Islamic State Blowing Up Iraq's Tomb of Jonah," National Public Radio, July 25, 2014, http://www.npr.org/blogs/thetwoway/2014/07/25/335192229/video-shows-islamic-state-blowing-up-iraqs-tomb-of-jonah.

74. Mark Movsesian, "Why Did ISIS Destroy the Tomb of Jonah?" *First Things*, July 2014, http://www.firstthings.com/blogs/firstthoughts/2014/07/why-did-isis-destroy-the-tomb-of-jonah.

75. Justin Moyer, "After Leveling Iraq's Tomb of Jonah, the Islamic State Could Destroy 'Anything in the Bible,'" *Washington Post*, July 25, 2014, http://www.washingtonpost.com/news/morning-mix/wp/2014/07/25/after-leveling-iraqs-tomb-ofjonah-the-islamic-state-could-destroy-anything-in-the-bible/?tid=hp_mm.

76. Eyder Peralta, "Video Shows Islamic State Blowing Up Iraq's Tomb of Jonah."

Chapter Six

77. Jeremy Bender, "Here's the New Kurdish Country That Could Emerge Out of the Iraq Crisis," Business Insider, June 19, 2014, http://www.businessinsider.com/heres-a-map-of-the-kurdish-nation-2014-6#ixzz3HuXRdhUU.

78. Alexandra Di Stefano Pironti, "Foreign Investment in Kurdistan at $5.5 Billion; UAE Among Top Investors," Rudaw, January 22, 2014, http://rudaw.net/english/business/22012014.

79. Sophie Jane Evans and Associated Press reporter, "Shocking Moment: ISIS Militants Take Sledgehammers to Mosul Tomb of Prophet Jonah as More Than 50 Blindfolded Bodies Area Found Massacred South of Baghdad," *Daily Mail*, July 9, 2014, http://www.dailymail.co.uk/news/article-2685923/

Shockingmoment-ISIS-militants-sledgehammers-Mosul-tomb-Prophet-Jonah-50-blindfolded-bodiesmassacred-south-Baghdad.html#ixzz3HgM2U5Q7.

80. Ibid.

81. Ibid.

82. Isak Nilsson, personal communication with the author, November 2, 2014.

83. Erik Prince and Glenn Beck, "Black Leaders Turn on Obama and Democrats," *The Glenn Beck Program*, October, 29, 2014, https://soundcloud.com/glennbeck/black-leaders-turn-on-obama-dems-102914.

84. Dexter Filkins, "The Fight of Their Lives," *New Yorker*, September 29, 2014, http://www.newyorker.com/magazine/2014/09/29/fight-lives.

Chapter Seven

85. Michael Gryboski, "Activists Applaud President Obama's Focus on Imprisoned Christians Abroad at National Prayer Breakfast," *Christian Post*, February 7, 2014, http://www.christianpost.com/news/activists-applaud-president-obamas-focus-on-imprisoned-christians-abroad-at-national-prayer-breakfast-114174/.

86. Tatiana Lozano, "ISIS Terrorists Threaten Life of American Pastor Imprisoned in Iran," CNS (Cybercast News Service), August 15, 2014, http://cnsnews.com/news/article/tatiana-lozano/isis-terrorists-threaten-life-american-pastor-imprisoned-iran.

87. "Iraq: ISIS Executed Hundreds of Prison Inmates," Human Rights Watch, October 30, 2014, http://www.hrw.org/news/2014/10/30/iraq-isis-executed-hundreds-prison-inmates.

88. "ACLJ Calls for Release of Iranian-American Christian Pastor Imprisoned in Iran Because of His Religious Beliefs," ACLJ.org, http://aclj.org/iran/aclj-calls-for-release-of-iranian-american-christian-pastor-imprisoned-in-iran-because-of-his-religious-beliefs.

89. "President Obama Discusses Saeed at Prayer National Breakfast," February 5, 2015, https://www.youtube.com/watch?v=xybNq-oG3LM.

90. Avi Asher-Schapiro, "Who Are the Yazidis, the Ancient, Persecuted Religious Minority Struggling to Survive in Iraq?" *National Geographic News*, August 9, 2014, http://news.nationalgeographic.com/news/2014/08/140809-iraq-yazidis-minority-isil-religion-history/.

91. Mary Chastain, "ISIS Buries 500 Yazidis Alive, Orders Others to Convert to Islam or Die," Breitbart News Network, August 10, 2014, http://www.breitbart.com/national-security/2014/08/10/isis-executes-at-least-500-yazidis-burying-many-alive-told-others-to-convert-to-islam-or-die/.

92. Samuel Smith, "Report: Islamic State Sells Yazidi Girls for $1,000, Yazidi Boys Forced to Train to Become ISIS Militants," *Christian Post*, October 13, 2014, http://www.christianpost.com/news/report-islamic-state-sells-yazidi-girls-for-1000-yazidi-boys-forced-to-train-to-become-isis-militants-127995/.

93. Ibid.

94. John Hall, "'I've Been Raped 30 Times and It's Not Even Lunchtime': Desperate Plight of Yazidi Woman Who Begged West to Bomb Her Brothel After ISIS Militants Sold Her into Sex Slavery," *Daily Mail*, October 21, 2014, http://www.dailymail.co.uk/news/article-2801353/i-ve-raped-30-times-s-not-lunchtime-desperate-plight-yazidi-woman-begged-west-bomb-brothel-isis-militants-sold-sex-slavery.html#ixzz3HhBasnVy.

95. Ibid.

96. Gary Lane, "New Iraqi Christian: ISIS Brutality a Turn Off to Islam," CBN News, August 31, 2014, http://www.cbn.com/cbnnews/world/2014/August/Northern-Iraq-is-facing-a-refugee-crisis-with-an-estimated-182000-Yazidis-fleeing-to-Kurdistan-to-escape-the-brutal-Islamic-State-ISIS-army-/.

Chapter Eight

97. "Sweden Becomes First EU Country to Recognise the Palestinian State," Euronews, October 10, 2014, http://www.euronews.com/2014/10/30/sweden-becomes-first-eu-country-to-recognise-the-palestinian-state/.

98. Dan Shuster, "Dan Shuster: Roadblocks to peace," Michigan Daily, April 5, 2005.

99. http://www.fbi.gov/about-us/investigate/terrorism/terrorism-definition.

100. "Yassir Arafat: 1929–2004," HonestReporting, November 11, 2004, http://honestreporting.com/yassir-arafat-1929-2004-2/.

101. "1983 Beirut Barracks Bombings," *Encyclopedia Britannica*, last modified September 3, 2013, http://global.britannica.com/EBchecked/topic/1474033/1983-Beirut-barracks-bombings.

102. "Burial Rites Put End to 7 1/2-Year Hostage Ordeal," *Los Angeles Times*, December 31, 1991), http://articles.latimes.com/1991-12-31/news/mn-1194_1_hostage-ordeal.

103. Irwin Cotler, "Why Hezbollah Is a Terrorist Organization," *Jerusalem Post*, July 18, 2013, http://www.jpost.com/Opinion/Op-Ed-Contributors/Why-Hezbollah-is-a-terrorist-organization-320297.

104. Ian Black, "UK Ready for Talks with Hezbollah," *Guardian*, March 4, 2009, http://www.theguardian.com/world/2009/mar/05/uk-set-for-hezbollah-talks.

105. Luke Coffey and James Phillips, *On Hezbollah, the U.S. Should Work Around the EU*, The Heritage Foundation May 10, 2013, http://www.heritage.org/research/reports/2013/05/europeanunion-should-designate-hezbollah-as-a-terrorist-organization.

106. Jean Aziz, "UN Envoy Meets with Hezbollah to Discuss Syria," Al-Monitor, October 22, 2014, http://www.al-monitor.com/pulse/originals/2014/10/hezbollah-role-syria-un-discussions.html.

107. "Hamas Charter (1988)," The Avalon Project, http://avalon.law.yale.edu/20th_century/hamas.asp.

108. Ibid.

109. Ibid.

110. David Adesnik, "Jimmy Carter Calls for Recognizing Hamas 'Legitimacy,'" Forbes, August 6, 2014, http://www.forbes.com/sites/davidadesnik/2014/08/06/jimmy-carter-calls-for-recognizing-hamas-legitimacy/.

111. Alexander Marquardt, "Hamas Praises Jerusalem Terrorist Attack," ABC News, November 5, 2014, http://abcnews.go.com/International/hamas-praisesjerusalem-terror-attack/story?id=26709425.

112. "Palestine Authority Funds Terrorists," Israel Ministry of Foreign Affairs, June 25, 2014, http://mfa.gov.il/MFA/ForeignPolicy/Terrorism/Palestinian/Pages/Palestinian-Authority-funds-terrorists-June-2014.aspx/.

113. Ibid.

114. Edwin Black quoted in Erick Stakelbeck, "Cash for Killers: US Funding Palestinian Terrorists?" CBN News, June 29, 2014, http://www.cbn.com/cbnnews/insideisrael/2014/June/Cash-for-Killers-US-Funding-Palestinian-Terrorists/.

115. Ibid.

Chapter Nine

116. Madeline Grant, "16% of French Citizens Support ISIS, Poll Finds," *Newsweek*, August 26, 2014, http://www.newsweek.com/16-french-citizens-support-isis-poll-finds-266795.

117. "Trojan Horse: ISIS Militants Come to Europe Disguised as Refugees, US Intel Source Claims," *Russia Today*. October 6, 2014, http://rt.com/news/193400-isis-militants-pose-refugees/.

118. "CNN: Finland Tops List of Countries with Muslim Fighters in Syria," *Yleisradio*, February 9, 2014, http://yle.fi/uutiset/cnn_finland_tops_list_of_countries_with_muslim_fighters_in_syria/7446816.

119. Nadette De Visser, "ISIS's Black Flags Are Flying in Europe," *Daily Beast*, July 28, 2014, http://www.thedailybeast.com/articles/2014/07/27/isis-s-black-flags-are-flying-in-europe.html.

120. http://www.ibtimes.co.uk/isis-master-plan-revealed-islamic-caliphate-will-rule-spain-china-balkans-1463782.

121. Sam Webb, "Sharia Law to Be Enshrined in British Legal System as Lawyers Get Guidelines on Drawing Up Documents According to Islamic Rules," *Daily Mail*, March 23, 2014, http://www.dailymail.co.uk/news/article-2587215/Sharia-Law-enshrined-British-legal-lawyersguidelines-drawing-documents-according-Islamic-rules.html.

122. Matt Danielsson, "Swedish Police Release Extensive Report Detailing Control of 55 'No-Go Zones' by Muslim Criminal Gangs," *Daily Caller*,

November 2, 2014, http://dailycaller.com/2014/11/02/swedish-police-release-extensive-report-detailing-control-of-55-no-go-zones-by-muslim-criminal-gangs/.

123. Richard Orange, "Swedish Riots Spark Surprise and Anger," *Guardian*, May 25, 2013, http://www.theguardian.com/world/2013/may/25/sweden-europe-news.

124. Michael Haltman, "As Muslim Population Grows, What Can Happen to a Society?" *Examiner*, June 23, 2010, http://www.examiner.com/article/as-muslim-population-grows-what-can-happen-to-a-society.

125. Ibid.

126. Modification of list compiled by TheReligionofPeace.com. Visit http://www.thereligionofpeace.com/pages/opinion-polls.htm.

127. http://gatesofvienna.net/2014/08/isis-in-sweden./

128. Mel Robbins, "Call Oklahoma Beheading What It Is: Terrorism," CNN News, September, 30, 2014, http://www.cnn.com/2014/09/30/opinion/robbins-oklahoma-nolen/.

129. Ryan Perry, "Muslim Convert 'Who Beheaded Colleague' Is Charged with Murder as It Emerges He Returned to Oklahoma Food Plant for 'Revenge' After He Was Fired Earlier That Day for 'Not Liking White People,'" *Daily Mail*, September 30, 2014, http://www.dailymail.co.uk/news/article-2775194/Oklahoma-man-charged-murder-beheading.html.

130. Ibid.

131. "Facebook Profile of Alton Nolen and the Signs of Radicalization," Insight Blog on Terrorism and Extremism, September 29, 2014, http://news.siteintelgroup.com/blog/index.php/entry/291-facebook-profile-of-alton-nolen-and-thesigns-of-radicalization.

132. Bill Hoffmann, "Muslim Whistleblower: Alton Nolen's Mosque Taught Hatred," Newsmax, October 7, 2014, http://www.newsmax.com/Newsfront/oklahoma-beheading-mosqueviolence/2014/10/07/id/599205/#ixzz3ISag47Ivr.

Chapter Ten

133. Alessandria Masi, "ISIS Recruiting Westerners: How the 'Islamic State' Goes After Non-Muslims and Recent Converts in the West," *International Business Times*, September 8, 2014, http://www.ibtimes.com/isis-recruiting-westerners-how-islamic-state-goes-after-non-muslims-recent-converts-west-1680076.

134. Ibid.

135. Samuel Smith, "Are African Americans Being Recruited by ISIS?" *Christian Post*, August 24, 2014, http://www.christianpost.com/news/are-african-americans-being-recruited-by-isis-125250/.

136. "Imam Receives Death Threat, Says ISIS Recruiting in Canada," *Al Arabiya News*, August 23, 2014, http://english.alarabiya.net/en/News/middle-east/2014/08/23/Imam-receives-death-threat-says-ISIS-recruiting-in-Canada.html.

137. "Islamic State Recruitment Soaring in Wake of U.S. Bombing," *Haaretz*, September 19, 2014, http://www.haaretz.com/news/middle-east/1.616730.

138. Pierre Thomas and Mike Levine, "New York Man Charged with Trying to Recruit ISIS Fighters in US," ABC News, September 16, 2014, http://abcnews.go.com/US/york-man-charged-recruit-isis-fighters-us/story?id=25552426.

139. Aaron Klein, "Blowback! U.S. Trained Islamists Who Joined ISIS," WND, June 17, 2014, http://www.wnd.com/2014/06/officials-u-s-trained-isis-at-secret-base-in-jordan/.

140. Cassandra Vinograd, Ghazi Balkiz, and Ammar Cheikh Omar, "ISIS Trains Child Soldiers at Camps for 'Cubs of the Islamic State,'" November 7, 2014, http://www.nbcnews.com/storyline/isis-terror/isis-trains-child-soldiers-camps-cubs-islamic-state-n241821; "Secret ISIS Scouts: Be Trained as 'Human Bombs' to Donate Blood for the Wounded," Netease International News, November 3, 2014, http://www.enews163.com/2014/11/03/secret-isis-scouts-be-trained-as-human-bombs-to-donate-blood-for-the-wounded-89633.html.

141. Nabih Bulos, Patrick J. McDonnell, and Raja Abdulrahim, "ISIS Weapons Windfall May Alter Balance in Iraq, Syria Conflicts," *LA Times*, June 29, 2014, http://www.latimes.com/world/middleeast/la-fg-iraq-isis-arms-20140629-story.html#page=1.

142. "US Probing Claims ISIS Fighters Seized Airdropped Weapons Meant for Kurds," Fox News, October 21, 2014, http://www.foxnews.com/politics/2014/10/21/us-probing-claims-isis-fighters-seized-airdropped-weapons-meant-for-kurds/.

143. Jeremy Bender, "As ISIS Routs the Iraqi Army, Here's a Look at What the Jihadists Have in Their Arsenal," *Business Insider*, July 8, 2014, http://www.businessinsider.com/isis-military-equipment-breakdown-2014-7?op=1.

144. Bryan Bender, "Stolen US-Made Equipment a Key Focus in ISIS Fight," *Boston Globe*, September 23, 2014, http://www.bostonglobe.com/news/world/2014/09/23/attacking-islamic-state-key-focus-for-stolen-american-made-equipment/EnGm9C5ZwebnQ60oowP5iM/story.html.

145. Ewen MacAskill, "Islamic State Training Pilots to Fly MiG Fighter Planes, Says Monitoring Group," *Guardian*, October 17, 2014, http://www.theguardian.com/world/2014/oct/17/islamic-state-training-pilots-mig-planes-syria.

146. Bruce Dorminey, "Ebola as ISIS Bio-Weapon?" *Forbes*, October 5, 2014, http://www.forbes.com/sites/brucedorminey/2014/10/05/ebola-as-isis-bio-weapon/.

147. Alexander Smith, "Nuclear Experts Play Down Threat of Uranium Stolen by ISIS," NBC News, July 10, 2014, http://www.nbcnews.com/storyline/iraq-turmoil/nuclear-experts-play-down-threat-uranium-stolen-isis-n152926.

148. Helen Lock, "ISIS Plans to Seize Iran's Nuclear Secrets, Attack Caviar Industry, Ruin Carpets," *Independent*, October 5, 2014, http://www.independent.

co.uk/news/world/middle-east/isis-manifesto-reveals-islamic-states-plans-to-seize-irans-nuclear-secrets-attack-caviar-industry-ruin-afghan-carpets-9775418.html.

149. Johnlee Varghese, "Shocking: ISIS Official 'Slave' Price List Shows Yazidi, Christian Girls Aged '1 to 9' Being Sold for $172," *International Business Times,* November 5, 2014, http://www.ibtimes.co.in/shocking-isis-official-slave-price-list-shows-yazidi-christian-girls-aged-1-9-being-sold-613160.

150. Ibid.

151. "UK Female Jihadists Run ISIS Sex-Slave Brothels," *Al Arabiya News,* September 12, 2014), http://english.alarabiya.net/en/variety/2014/09/12/UK-female-jihadists-run-ISIS-sex-slave-brothels.html.

152. Ibid.

153. Abdelhak Mamoun, "ISIS Document Sets Prices of Christian and Yazidi Slaves," *Iraqi News,* November 3, 2014, http://www.iraqinews.com/features/exclusive-isis-document-sets-prices-christian-yazidi-slaves/.

154. "Muslims Rape over 300 Swedish Children and 700 Women in First 7 Months of 2013," *Muslim Issue,* October 13, 2014, https://themuslimissue.wordpress.com/2013/10/13/muslims-raped-over-300-swedish-children-and-700-women-in-seven-months-of-2013/.

155. Tsvi Sadan, "Let's Talk About Sweden," *Israel Today,* October 6, 2014, http://www.israeltoday.co.il/NewsItem/tabid/178/nid/25390/Default.aspx.

Chapter Eleven

156. "Global Christianity—A Report on the Size and Distribution of the World's Christian Population," Pew Research Center, December 19, 2011, http://www.pewforum.org/2011/12/19/global-christianity-exec/.

157. David Barrett and Todd M. Johnson, *World Christian Trends* (Pasadena, CA: William Carey Library, 2013).

158. Todd M. Johnson, *Status of Global Missions 2013,* cited in Walter Pavlo, "Fraud Thriving in U.S. Churches, But You Wouldn't Know It," *Forbes,* November 18, 2013, http://www.forbes.com/sites/walterpavlo/2013/11/18/fraud-thriving-in-u-s-churches-but-you-wouldnt-know-it/.

159. Mats Tunehag, "A Global Overview of the Business as Mission Movement: Needs & Gaps," *Lausanne World Pulse*: 1 (2009), http://www.lausanneworldpulse.com/perspectives.php/1074?pg=all.

160. Ibid.

Chapter Twelve

161. Gary Lane, "New Iraqi Christian: ISIS Brutality a Turn Off to Islam."

162. "ISIS Causes Iraqis to Turn to Christ at a 'Stunning Pace,'" *Breaking Christian News,* October 10, 2014, http://www.breakingchristiannews.com/articles/display_art.html?ID=14747.

About the Author

Eugene Bach is a pseudonym for a member of the Chinese underground church who does not wish to be identified. He has been working with the underground church in China for more than fifteen years, helping its members to establish forward mission bases in closed countries around the world, including Iraq and Syria. Eugene leads the Chinese mission movement called *Back to Jerusalem,* which provides essential support for Chinese missionaries in Africa, Asia, and the Middle East. He has written books about the underground church in China, North Korea, and Iran.